ADOPTED BY AN AWESOME FATHER

JoAnne Thompson

authorHOUSE®

AuthorHouse™ UK
1663 Liberty Drive
Bloomington, IN 47403 USA
www.authorhouse.co.uk
Phone: 0800.197.4150

Scripture quotations marked NIV are taken from the Holy Bible, New
International Version. NIV. Copyright 1973, 1978, 1984 by International
Bible Society. Used by permission of Zondervan. All rights reserved.

Scripture quotations marked RSV are taken from the Revised Standard Version of
the Bible, copyright 1946, 1952, 1971 by the Division of Christian Education of the
National Council of the Churches of Christ in the USA. Used by permission.

Published by AuthorHouse 11/16/2016

ISBN: 978-1-5246-6480-0 (sc)
ISBN: 978-1-5246-6481-7 (hc)
ISBN: 978-1-5246-6482-4 (e)

For my amazing family, especially my awesome dad, who
showed me what a loving father is.

CONTENTS

Study Guide on the Theology of Adoption

THE PURPOSE OF this short study guide is to enable those who are studying to be local preachers within the Methodist Church, or preachers in other denominations, to more clearly understand the theology of adoption.

Personal stories, illustrations, and discussion questions are used in order to help those who have this privilege of preaching, teaching, and leading worship, to relate this foundational yet often overlooked subject to their own lives, congregations, and groups or individuals that they minister to or work alongside, that they in turn will enable others to hear, know, and accept the amazing and awesome love of God that this subject presents to us.

When I was asked to write this, the person asking didn't know I was adopted, and my initial concern was that relating my own experiences would be emotionally difficult for many people involved in my story, including myself. However, it has been a privilege to relate this subject to my own experience. I have an amazingly supportive family who have been encouraging and honest with me about their feelings, and for this I am really grateful. It has also reinforced the assurance of God's faithfulness and grace towards me.

My hope is that this book will help you understand how God's desire for us all is to be adopted into his family and what that actually means for our lives. I hope what I've written will be helpful in your ministry to others who may struggle with understanding their spiritual adoption as a child of the living God

At the end of each section are questions that can be considered either individually or as a group. They are there to help you think about some of the points I raise. For some, these will not be helpful, but for others, they may help you examine more deeply your relationship with God thus enabling you to more effectively introduce people to God as their Father.

ACKNOWLEDGEMENTS

THANKS ARE DUE to those Methodist local preachers in training who have encouraged me to produce this short book and for those who have supported and encouraged me for thirty years as a Methodist local preacher and tutor.

Thanks to Jeff, Joel, and Laura for their encouragement, and thanks to my church family at New Life Church in Newcastle upon Tyne for their willingness to read and make suggestions about my book. I thank them for all their prayers and support over the last two years.

INTRODUCTION

I GREW UP in a very loving, very secure family, a family which, looking back, was probably something of a dying breed – a working-class urban family in Leeds, West Yorkshire. I was part of an extended family where aunties, uncles, and cousins were very important and everyone had a part to play and shared advice about raising each other's children. We all lived close to each other, with the exception of the Otley cousins. When we were little, we thought they lived in a different country because they lived all of twelve miles away.

Christmas and family events were celebrated with family parties and visits to the aunties and uncles, and as I and my sister were the youngest of fourteen cousins, we were 'looked after' by our older cousins, who tried to impart their 'wisdom' to us!

It was a family that celebrated each other's achievements and rallied round to help each other when needed. My grandma was very much the matriarch. Two of my uncles and my dad worked together in the same factory along with various other members of the family.

Holidays were shared together; weekends and days out were shared, and we even went on the Friday food shop together to the Gem, a supermarket where the mums met the dads after work on a Friday to get the money straight from their wage packets to do the weekly shop.

We all knew which aunties and uncles would give us sympathy if we were in trouble with our parents, and we knew which ones wouldn't. We knew how we were expected to behave in each other's houses and what we could and couldn't get away with.

Like all families, ours had its ups and downs; people fell out with each other, and there were disagreements, but as a child, I considered our family normal. We were brought up with a clear idea of right and wrong and were made very aware if we overstepped the mark.

We shared common interests and passions. For instance, it wouldn't have been proper if we supported any other football team than Leeds United (the greatest football team in all the land!).

The notion that family was important was always there, and it was encouraged and instilled in us. To this day that sense of family is still extremely important. Even our children and grandchildren are friends on Facebook, and we keep linked with our cousins this way, celebrating each other's achievements and sharing in each other's sadness and heartaches. We still have the occasional family parties and get-togethers.

It is with this background that I write this short book and study notes.

I realize that some of my friends and acquaintances, some of whom were adopted and some who were raised by biological parents, were not all blessed with a family like mine. I am therefore very thankful to God for the family he chose me to be part of and to the family who chose me to be part of them.

CHAPTER 1

Our Father

JESUS TAUGHT US when praying to address God as our Father.

I often hear people talk about how they find it difficult to relate to God as their Father because they didn't have such a good earthly father, or perhaps their father died, or they never knew their father. I would contend that this has been the same throughout history – that parents have not always got it right but God has made a way for us all to have the perfect Father. God our Father will never let us down or leave us or give up on us. Our parents are given a massive responsibility to raise us, but our heavenly Father is the one Jesus points us to as the one in whom we should put our trust.

How can it be that such an awesome, amazing God, the God of the whole universe could possibly want a relationship with us? Is it actually possible?

The Bible says that if you have placed your trust in Jesus, then you have been adopted by the Father, the God of the whole universe. You are his child. He will give you his name, protection, provision, inheritance, and most importantly, his love. This is not to be taken lightly. It is an amazing gift, and one that many people find hard to grasp and accept.

The Bible tells us in Romans 8:14–16, 'For as many as are led by the Spirit of God, these are the sons of God. For you did not receive the spirit of bondage again to fear, but you received the Spirit of adoption by whom we cry out, "Abba, Father". The Spirit bears witness with our spirit that we are children of God'.

We are not God's foster children. We are his children, and all the intimacy this suggests is ours if we want it.

Galatians 3:26 says, 'For you are all sons of God through faith in Christ Jesus'.

Ephesians 1:5 tells us: 'He predestined us to adoption as sons through Jesus Christ to himself, in accordance with his pleasure and will'.

Additionally, there are familiar verses, such as John 3:16: 'For God so loved the world that he gave his only son so that whoever believes in him will not die but have eternal life'.

They remind us that those who trust Jesus are destined to live forever with God.

But however great that is, it's not the whole story. We also enter into a Father-child relationship in the present, with all the benefits and privileges of being a child of the living God. We get him to love us, protect us, and provide for us, and we get to know him intimately as our Father.

When Jesus was teaching the disciples the Lord's Prayer, they were hearing a different sort of prayer from the one they were used to hearing. They were compelled to ask Jesus to teach them how to pray in an intimate way, to pray to God as an approachable Father: accessible, relational, and near, affirming them as his sons yet being Holy. The prayer Jesus teaches is not about the majesty of God, and it's not about protocol, and there is no suggestion of distance between those praying it and God himself, just a loving caring relationship.

One of the most important purposes of the Bible, the Word of God, is to tell us about the nature of this relationship between the created and the Creator. Those who see the Bible as a list of rules or guidelines are missing the point and the good news in it. It's a love letter from God, where he reveals himself by telling his people, over and over, of his love for us. He chose us.

It is important to understand and know what God thinks of us and how he sees us and accept this for ourselves if we are to share that knowledge and that love with others. The Bible tells us God's heart for us.

Barry Adams put together this 'Father's Love Letter', a series of paraphrased Bible verses, which says it all:

My dear Child, you may not know me, but I know everything about you (Psalm 139:1).

I know when you sit down and when you rise up (Psalm 139:2).

I am familiar with all your ways (Psalm 139:3).

Even the very hairs on your head are numbered (Matthew 10:29–31).

For you were made in my image (Genesis 1:27).

In me you live and move and have your being (Acts 17:28).

For you are my offspring (Acts 17:28).

I knew you even before you were conceived (Jeremiah 1:4–5).

I chose you when I planned creation (Ephesians 1:11–12).

You were not a mistake, for all your days are written in my book (Psalm 139:15–16).

I determined the exact time of your birth and where you would live (Acts 17:26).

You are fearfully and wonderfully made (Psalm 139:14). I knit you together in your mother's womb (Psalm 139:13). And brought you forth on the day you were born (Psalm 71:6). I have been misrepresented by those who don't know me (John 8:41–44).

I am not distant and angry, but am the complete expression of love (1 John 4:16).

And it is my desire to lavish my love on you (1 John 3:1). Simply because you are my child and I am your father (1 John 3:1).

I offer you more than your earthly father ever could (Matthew 7:11).

For I am the perfect father (Matthew 5:48).

Every good gift that you receive comes from my hand (James 1:17).

For I am your provider and I meet all your needs (Matthew 6:31–33).

My plan for your future has always been filled with hope (Jeremiah 29:11).

Because I love you with an everlasting love (Jeremiah 31:3).

My thoughts toward you are countless as the sand on the seashore (Psalm 139:17–18).

And I rejoice over you with singing (Zephaniah 3:17).

I will never stop doing good to you (Jeremiah 32:40).

For you are my treasured possession (Exodus 19:5).

I desire to establish you with all my heart and all my soul (Jeremiah 32:41).

And I want to show you great and marvellous things (Jeremiah 33:3).

If you seek me with all your heart, you will find me (Deuteronomy 4:29).

Delight in me and I will give you the desires of your heart (Psalm 37:4).

For it is I who gave you those desires (Philippians 2:13).

I am able to do more for you than you could possibly imagine (Ephesians 3:20).

For I am your greatest encourager (2 Thessalonians 2:16–17).

I am also the Father who comforts you in all your troubles (2 Corinthians 1:3–4).

When you are broken-hearted, I am close to you (Psalm 34:18).

As a shepherd carries a lamb, I have carried you close to my heart (Isaiah 40:11).

One day I will wipe away every tear from your eyes (Revelation 21:3–4).

And I'll take away all the pain you have suffered on this earth (Revelation 21:3–4).

I am your Father, and I love you even as I love my son, Jesus (John 17:23).

For in Jesus, my love for you is revealed (John 17:26).

He is the exact representation of my being (Hebrews 1:3).

He came to demonstrate that I am for you, not against you (Romans 8:31).

And to tell you that I am not counting your sins (2 Corinthians 5:18–19).

Jesus died so that you and I could be reconciled (2 Corinthians 5:18–19).

His death was the ultimate expression of my love for you (1 John 4:10).

I gave up everything I loved that I might gain your love (Romans 8:31–32).

If you receive the gift of my son Jesus, you receive me (1 John 2:23).

And nothing will ever separate you from my love again (Romans 8:38–39).

Come home and I'll throw the biggest party heaven has ever seen (Luke 15:7).

I have always been Father, and will always be Father (Ephesians 3:14–15).

My question is, Will you be my child? (John 1:12–13).

I am waiting for you (Luke 15:11–32).

Love, your Dad,
Almighty God[1]

Points to Consider

1. What are the main problems that members of your congregation may have with the concept of seeing God as their Father?

2. The New Testament seems to have a very different idea of the relationship between God and his creation from the one presented in the Old Testament. Make a list of well-known Bible stories of God interacting with people. Describe the relationships between God and the people in these stories. By calling God our Father, are we being too familiar with God? Are we demonstrating a lack of 'reverence' or 'respect'?

3. In 'The Father's Love Letter', what do you think are the three most important things God is saying to you about what he thinks about you? Try to choose three verses from 'The Fathers Love Letter' each week and meditate, pray, and think about them; let them seep into your heart.
   When you understand these for yourself and can accept them, you'll be able to share them with others more effectively. Don't be afraid to ask other Christians whom you trust, for help. The body of Christ is there to build each other up and

---

[1] Wendy Thomas, *Walking with God as Father*, foreword by Barry Adams, UK: New Wine Press, 2013.

support each other. Some things will be hard to grasp because we are all broken people.

4. Try writing a love letter to God to tell him how you feel about him. Then use this as a basis for your prayers of thanks, praise, and adoration within a service that you lead.

5. Watch 'A Father's Love Letter' on YouTube (https://www.youtube.com/watch?v=WYzr3JavFqM) and consider how you could use this in an act of worship.

CHAPTER 2

The Search for Truth

I WAS 24 years old, married, and had just had my first child, Joel. My uncle was researching our family tree, a passion I shared. I was fascinated by the whole history thing but I also wanted to solve a mystery. My grandmother never spoke about my mum's father despite the fact that she spent a lot of time telling us stories of her early life. Her stories made history come alive, but when it came to my mum's dad, there was nothing – no mention, not even a hint. My mum was brought up by her stepfather, and she wasn't all that interested in knowing about her biological father either. As far as she was concerned, her dad was the one who brought her up and provided for her, and she was secure in that. This wasn't something I understood at the time because I had no concept of what it meant to be adopted. Uncle Syd was well on with my dad's side of the family, so I got to work on my mum's, trying to solve the mystery.

I found out lots of things about the history of my mother's family. Nothing was all that spectacular. I visited places my grandma had told me about, searched through lots of family history records, visited lots of cemeteries, and tried to imagine how my family coped with the harsh realities of industrial Leeds. I took photos and made notes but never really found what I was looking for.

I unearthed things that someone living in a different century might view as tragic. My grandmother was adopted by her grandmother and then her aunt, because her parents died – or so she had been led to believe. The truth was, her mother remarried after her dad and younger sister died. My grandmother was only 2 years old. Her mother's new husband didn't want to be burdened with a small child, so she was left with her grandmother. I wonder now whether this was partly why my grandmother was close to me, because she had been adopted at a young age as well.

There was a thrill and an excitement knowing I was part of a bigger picture, part of a history of two families coming together, but it was so difficult to see where my love of books and study came from. Personality-wise I was very much like my dad, and like all teenage girls I clashed with my mum on most things and argued with my sister, who was so very different from me that it's amazing neither of us ever suspected what I was soon to find out.

On one occasion I took the information that I'd collected round to my uncle's house, and his wife, Auntie Mavis, seeing my enthusiasm, said to me, 'If I were you I wouldn't bother with things in the past; you might find out something that you don't want to know'.

This of course made me think there really was something to find out about my mother's family.

As children, most of us have a natural curiosity to find out the truth about things, about how things work. We ask questions, because we want and need to know. If you have ever had or looked after children, you'll know that phase they go through (which drives you crazy!) when they ask 'why?' about everything: Why do we have to? Why does this happen? Why aren't we there yet? And even with the most patient of parents, their answer eventually ends up being, 'Because I said so!'

The Bible is full of the 'why?' questions, especially if you read through the book of Psalms. There are heartfelt pleas to God for answers to big questions, a sense that God wants us to ask the questions, but also the peace that is found when the writer comes to the conclusion that even when they can't understand the answer, even when it doesn't make sense, it is good because, 'God says so!'

If you read Psalm 42, it's full of the big questions of life, even 'Where is God?' But it finishes with 'Put your hope in God, for I will yet praise him, my saviour and my God'.

Even from the cross Jesus himself asks, 'My God, my God, why have you forsaken me? *Eloi, Eloi lama sabachthani?"* (Matthew 27:46).

Every year during the Passover meal in a Jewish household, the story of the exodus will be recounted at the Seder meal, the youngest boy of the family will ask the questions, 'Why? Why on this night do we ...?'

It's important for Jewish children to ask these questions and for the head of the house to answer them.

God gave us brains and curiosity and allows us to make our own choices; without asking the questions and considering the answers, we can't really make a choice. In the Bible God presents us with choices, but he also expects us to ask the questions.

John 3 is a great example of this. Nicodemus questions Jesus: 'Well, what does it mean to be born again?'

How can this happen? What is it all about?

Joshua 24:15 says, 'Decide this day whom you will serve'. Without asking the questions, how can you make a decision as to whom you will serve?

In order to make those decisions, we need to be able to ask questions to find out, to be curious. We encourage children to explore, to work things out so they learn.

However, there are times when we don't understand yet what it's all about and don't know the answers. Then we have to trust that God knows what he is doing because he said so! Children have to learn to understand that their parents want the best for them. We can tell a 3-year-old that he or she has to eat vegetables because it's good for them, and the child might accept it at that level, but it's not the full answer. We only give the answer in terms that a 3-year-old will understand. If this is not an acceptable answer, going into a scientific explanation would be of no use; the 3-year-old would not understand anyway. Children need to accept and understand that their parents love them and want the best for them, and therefore, their word should be accepted. As they grow older, then it's right that they ask questions and learn more.

This is the same with us and God. God allows us to ask the questions, but sometimes we can't see or understand the answers; we learn as we grow. There are times that we have to just trust and accept that what God says is right and is in our best interests.

Many questions can be answered by looking at the past. I was able to answer some questions about my family by researching the past and listening to stories and looking at the evidence, but I couldn't find the answer to everything.

In the Bible we have a wonderful living history of God's dealings with his creation, a history of his relationship with us. We can ask questions about all sorts of things: What is the purpose of a wasp? for instance. Or why do bad things happen? In time we may learn the answers, but the questions about how God sees us and about his desire and purpose for our lives and what's in his heart for us is right there in the Bible.

Points to Consider

1. Is it a good thing to ask questions of God, or should we just trust him that he knows what he is doing?
2. What are the big life questions that people ask?
3. What scripture can you point people to in order to answer some of these questions?
4. When people struggle with life, what can you do or say to enable them to find the answers that they need from God?
5. Why do you think God allowed you to choose whether you wanted to follow him or not, whether you would be adopted or not?
6. What are the top ten questions that you would like to ask God? Make a list and see whether other people you know have the same or similar questions.

7. God wants to have a Father-child relationship with us. How does that make you feel?

8. Talk this through with close Christian friends. Then write a psalm in your own words in the same way that the psalmist does in Psalm 42. Discuss:

   1. why God is so good;
   2. what the questions are;
   3. what you think God's response would be; and
   4. your response to God.

9. Can you think of another story in the Bible like the exodus that you could tell children or discuss with adults? Perhaps you could ask questions that could be answered in a community event such as a meal or in a play or during a presentation.

CHAPTER 3

Finding the Truth

BY THIS TIME I had been doing my mum's family tree for a year or so. I had collected a number of birth, marriage, and death certificates and had placed them in an envelope together with my own birth certificate. Mine was a short version, so I decided to send for my full certificate from Leeds just to make things complete.

I sent a letter with the details of where and when I was born and enclosed my cheque. A few weeks later I received a letter and my cheque returned, saying no one of that name could be traced in the records. I was a little frustrated with this because I just thought they hadn't looked properly, so I rang up my friend Christine in Leeds and asked her whether she could go to the registry office and obtain it for me.

A few days later Christine rang and told me it definitely wasn't there. She then gently said, 'You don't suppose you were adopted, do you?' At that point, Christine realized I must have been adopted because this was the only possible explanation.

Without hesitation I said, 'Of course not. I would have known if I had been'.

She then said the registrar would be quite happy to go through the books with me if I wanted to make an appointment and come down to Leeds to see him. So I did.

On the day of the appointment I still had no idea what was about to happen. I was on my way to Spring Harvest and thought I would get this cleared up and pick up the certificate, which they were bound to have found by now, and we would be on our way.

As I walked through the door into the registry office, I saw one of my older cousins, Clive, sat waiting for his birth certificate – one of those God 'incidents' that seem to happen a lot. What were the chances of one of my cousins being in the registry office of a big city on exactly the same day at exactly the same time as I went in?

We hugged, and he asked me what I was doing there. I told him about how the Leeds registry office had somehow managed to lose the records of my birth.

He went a very pale colour and said, 'Jo, have they never told you?'

'Who? Told me what?'

'That you're adopted'.

It was one of those moments where time stands still and the reality of what you've just heard doesn't really sink in. He then told me I'd been adopted as a baby and that was why they couldn't find the certificate.

At that point the registrar took me into a small room and proceeded to tell me that they had found my birth certificate and that my name was JoAnne Cross at birth, not JoAnne Thompson, but that's all he could tell me. The rules at that time meant that in order to get the names of my birth parents, I would need to go through counselling first.

I came out still not believing I was actually someone different from who I thought I was. I was confident about my place within my family, and I was confident about my place in the history of my family. How could this be?

Clive waited for me to come out because he was worried about me. I told him I needed time to take it in and not to tell anyone that I knew, which he agreed to. I didn't even tell my husband or anyone, and I went to Spring Harvest while I desperately tried to work out what this actually meant for me.

When we are adopted, our identity is changed. When we are adopted by God and made his child, we are 'a new creation' (2 Corinthians 5:17). The old life, and the life before adoption, has gone, and we are made new. I lived for twenty-four years not knowing I was adopted. It was obvious by the way I was treated that this adoption had been complete in every way. There was never anything to suggest I was anything but my mum's and dad's daughter, but it was at this point in my life that I had to accept that adoption and try to work out what that meant for me and my identity. Who was I? The week after I found out was a time where I had to wrestle with who I was and other questions about my identity and God's purpose in this.

Getting clear on our identity often determines how we live. For example, if children are told often enough that they are bad, they start to believe it and act accordingly. I knew who I was in my family, but I had to work out who I was now.

People talk about what they do and where they have been but rarely talk about who they are. As Christians we can believe that we are God's precious children and that he holds us safely in his hands. We have to take God at his word, which then sets us free from believing anything else about ourselves other than being secure that we are accepted and loved by God and that he will give us all we ever need.

I had to ask the questions, why did God choose to create me in this way? Why couldn't I just be born naturally into my family? It seems like a bit of a long way round for God to get me where he wanted me to be. I would now have to work out who I was, who my parents were, and how I fit into my family and the world.

Points to Consider

> Pilate asked, 'What is truth?' Jesus said, 'I am the way, the truth, and the life' (John 14:6). Often, when we are preaching, God can challenge us about the things we have held to be true all our lives when we suddenly realize they're not true.

1. What is the truth about ourselves in relation to God? How could you help people who are questioning to know how to find truth?

    John Wesley, in his Sermon Number 9, 'The Spirit of Bondage and Adoption' (see appendix 4) talks about the natural man, the man under the law, and the man under grace. How do we help those who have gone from the 'natural man state' to the 'man under the law' and finally 'the man under grace'?

2. Try to think of a creative way of explaining what Wesley was trying to say in a way people in the twenty-first century can understand.

3. Think about a time in your life when you found out something that you always thought was secure and certain but turned out to not be so. Perhaps you found out about the death of someone close or were told information about something that completely changed how you saw things. Through your preaching, how can you help others in your congregation come to terms with their insecurity?

CHAPTER 4

It's All about Grace

IN MANY WAYS, although I tried to work things out, the fact was, the decision had already been made on my behalf. There was nothing to work out because legal things had happened that meant I was adopted. I was the child of my mum and dad; it was a fact. As a baby I'd been adopted. It wasn't my decision at all. However, once I'd learned I was adopted, I now had to make a decision whether I accepted this choice that had been made for me, the choice my parents made to adopt me as their own and love me unconditionally. Or I had to walk away to try to find my identity in something or somebody else.

This made me think back ten years prior, when I made a commitment to Jesus for the first time. I had been going to a Methodist church since I joined the Brownies at age 7, and no one ever said anything to me and my friends about making our own decisions to follow Christ, about becoming a Christian. We assumed and were led to believe that we were Christians already. We were encouraged to become church members at the age of 13 or 14. This was seen as our point of commitment to church, not to Jesus.

I remember, after becoming a member of the church and being asked to go on a committee, being congratulated by one of the stewards, who said, 'Congratulations! You're a real Methodist now you're on a committee!'

Making a decision to follow Jesus was never talked about. We just went to the church and were part of it because we went to Brownies or a youth club or whatever.

There is and always has been a need to recognise within the church that belonging is important, but if it just stops there and we never make a conscious decision to belong and remain, and we don't know why we belong, then it's easy to just walk away. All it is, really, is a club or an organisation that you can take or leave. It's not about a life-changing experience where we come to realize who we belong to, to realize what that means and to say, 'Yes, I want to belong. I want to belong to Jesus and be part of his family'.

It came as a shock to me and my friends when we went away on a circuit youth weekend and were challenged about whether we wanted to be Christians, to be told we had to make a decision and that our eternity depended on this. That the security we thought we had because we went to church and were part of the church family wasn't actually secure at all; wasn't actually all that secure until we came to a point of accepting Jesus as our Saviour, until we recognised God as our Father.

Within the Methodist church and many other denominations, children are brought up to believe they are children of God, are part of the church family, and so they are, but there is a danger here of being universalist. In the same way, when my mum and dad got me at ten days old, I became their child, but it wasn't until the adoption papers had been signed that I was legally their child. They accepted me and treated me as their child for that year, but there was always that chance that my birth parents could come back and get me. Until the papers were signed, it wasn't certain.

At a service of infant baptism or dedication, the parents make promises. Promises from the Bible are read, the church makes promises, and if the church and the parents keep those promises, the child will be nurtured and know he or she belongs to the family of God and is loved by God their Father. However, there is always a point where you must accept that place in the family and choose whether you are going to accept God as your father.

Jesus, by dying for us on the cross, made it possible for us to be adopted by God as his children. He gave us a way to have that same relationship that he had with his Father, but it's not until we 'hand over the papers', so to speak, that we sign our old life away and allow God to seal it with the blood of his son that we are really his. That is then adoption; it's a commitment that cannot be broken from the Father's side.

Once that adoption paper is signed, you're the child of your new parents. They're your parents forever. When we say yes to God and he adopts us into his family, we are his children, his heirs forever.

When you are born, you have the same genes or looks as your birth parents, but the input from around you, from being nurtured, is so very important. This is why, when children become part of our church during a baptism, dedication or thanksgiving service, and we stand up and make promises as their church family to support the parents in the Christian upbringing of a child, we are then responsible for keeping those promises and nurturing those children and providing the things that they need, providing a solid foundation in their lives until they come to that point of accepting Jesus for themselves.

Some of us as local preachers will be involved in talking to parents who bring their children to the church for baptism or a thanksgiving service. It is so important that we are not just concentrating on what happens on that one day but on the point of it all. This is a lifelong commitment by them and the church to nurture the children in the way of Christ, that they understand that there is a time when they must ensure that the children learn that they have to choose for themselves.

It is vitally important for people to also realize this truth: If I had walked away from my family and my parents when I found out about my adoption, it would not have made them any less my family or any less my parents. They were the ones who signed the adoption papers, the ones who wanted me and claimed me as their own. In the same way that God does this for all people, he chose to make us, to adopt us as his own. He signed the adoption papers with the blood of his son, Jesus. His love for us was unconditional, and it was all about his love for us. But there is a time when a decision has to be made as to whether we accept or reject that love.

This is the Grace of God. It's not about what we have done it about what God has done for us, what the hymn writer refers to as 'Amazing Grace'.

Within the congregations to whom you preach there will be many, who although they have been going to church all their lives will never have heard or realized this. It can be seen by some as a bit radical, a bit over the top, and it can come as a shock to people, and unsettling for some. They thought they were secure as members of a church suddenly they realise that actually their only security is in a relationship with God and nothing else.

In Luke 15:11–32, the Parable of the Lost Son (Prodigal Son) illustrates this:

> Jesus continued: 'There was a man who had two sons. The younger one said to his father, "Father, give me my share of the estate". So he divided his property between them.

> 'Not long after that, the younger son got together all he had, set off for a distant country, and there squandered his wealth in wild living. After he had spent everything, there was a severe famine in that whole country, and he began to be in need. So he went and hired himself out to a citizen of that country, who sent him to his fields to feed pigs. He longed to fill his stomach with the pods that the pigs were eating, but no one gave him anything.

> 'When he came to his senses, he said, "How many of my father's hired servants have food to spare, and here I am starving to death! I will set out and go back to my father and say to him: Father, I have sinned

against heaven and against you. I am no longer worthy to be called your son; make me like one of your hired servants". So he got up and went to his father.

'But while he was still a long way off, his father saw him and was filled with compassion for him; he ran to his son, threw his arms around him and kissed him.

'The son said to him, "Father, I have sinned against heaven and against you. I am no longer worthy to be called your son".

'But the father said to his servants, "Quick! Bring the best robe and put it on him. Put a ring on his finger and sandals on his feet. Bring the fattened calf and kill it. Let's have a feast and celebrate. For this son of mine was dead and is alive again; he was lost and is found". So they began to celebrate.

'Meanwhile, the older son was in the field. When he came near the house, he heard music and dancing. So he called one of the servants and asked him what was going on. "Your brother has come", he replied, "and your father has killed the fattened calf because he has him back safe and sound".

'The older brother became angry and refused to go in. So his father went out and pleaded with him. But he answered his father, "Look! All these years I've been slaving for you and never disobeyed your orders. Yet you never gave me even a young goat so I could celebrate with my friends. But when this son of yours who has squandered your property with prostitutes comes home, you kill the fattened calf for him!"

"'My son", the father said, "you are always with me, and everything I have is yours. But we had to celebrate and be glad, because this brother of yours was dead and is alive again; he was lost and is found"'.

Many people who have been going to church all their lives and have always thought of themselves as good church folk have not really understood how amazing the Father's love is because they have never been without it. They find it difficult, like the older son, to then accept those people coming back into the church who have left, who have gone astray and not been faithful. But the Father wants that relationship with everyone, and as Christians we should rejoice with God when one of his children comes home, rather than seeing it as a problem.

Points to Consider

1. As part of your local preacher's study, you will have looked at grace and what this means. How can you explain to your congregation the grace of God in the context of spiritual adoption?
2. Telling your story is important. Discuss the point where you accepted your spiritual adoption (do this as an elevator speech: you have three minutes!).
3. What difference does this adoption make in your life?
4. Create a leaflet for parents who want to have their child baptised or dedicated. Use pictures and diagrams or symbols which can illustrate and explain what they are about to do in the service on behalf of their child and what their responsibilities may be.

5. How can you explain to a congregation or person what the need for adoption is and why it needs to happen?

6. How would your church and you react if a group of people who may have a criminal background came in en masse and said they had become Christians? What if they started to get excited about Jesus and disrupted the service because they didn't know what was expected of them?

CHAPTER 5

Life before Adoption?

THERE IS OFTEN a difference between people like me who were adopted as babies and who were, therefore, just too young to know what life was like before adoption, and those who were adopted when they were older.

I used to work in a children's home. One of the young people there had spent most of his junior school days in isolation, was very troubled, and had tried desperately to cling to the idea that he had wonderful parents who would one day turn up for him. Of course they never did.

He was a lovely lad, but always appeared to be very sad and demanded a lot of attention from staff. We all knew this was something he needed and there wasn't anyone who didn't want someone to come along and adopt him. At 13 years old it was very unlikely. He had years of instability behind him, which would be hard for any prospective adopters, as well as for himself. Adoption would mean that he would have to let go of the notion that these parents who he had imagined were super parents would come and get him, and he would have to learn to see two other people as his parents.

The longer people live with the lack of understanding that God wants to adopt them, wants to be the one they rely on for everything, the harder it is. The older we get, the more we try to rely on no one else – just ourselves. We convince ourselves that we don't need anyone else and that we can manage on our own. This is untrue, because we were made for relationships, relationship with God and relationships with others. Relationships can be defined in lots of ways.

However, when people are adopted as an older child, they have an understanding of how precious that adoption is and how much their life has been made different by it.

One day, after getting into trouble, the young lad was brought back to the children's home by the police, and we noticed that he had struck up a friendship with the policeman who had brought him back. Within six months he started a foster placement with the policeman and his wife and was eventually adopted by them. We had a big party to celebrate, and the change in him was immediate. He was so desperate to have loving parents that he had no hesitation in calling them mam and dad. He knew he was adopted. He knew he was getting a new life, and he knew what it meant.

This young man knew his new mam and dad had picked him, wanted him personally even with all his troubled background and history. He was special.

In middle school, my English teacher asked us all to bring in something that was important to us and to speak about it. Most of us brought in things about our hobbies. I took in my city of Leeds Swimming Club track suit.

But one of my classmates brought his adoption certificate. He explained to the class that this was important to him because it meant that his mum and dad thought he was special because they had chosen him to be their child. By adopting him they had picked him as their son.

This was something my classmate was very proud of, and it was clear that it had been a really good thing that his parents had told him. By telling him that he was chosen specially, they were essentially telling him, 'You did not start out as a member of our family, but we chose to take you in as our own and make you our child. You get all the benefits and privileges that come with being our child. You get us to love you unconditionally, to teach and protect you, to take care of you and provide for you. You get our name, and you will be given an inheritance'.

Points to Consider

When we're born we can't make decisions for ourselves, so parents have to make those decisions for us. This includes how we will be brought up – where, how, and what sort of things we will do.

1. When you accepted that God was your Father, when you made that commitment to Christ, how did your life change?
2. How could you explain to a congregation how God adopted you as his child and what difference that made to your life?
3. If you were to show a congregation something that represented the most important thing that has happened in your life, what would it be?

CHAPTER 6

Living with the Truth

MY SISTER BROUGHT my nephew Paris (then about 4 years old) to Spring Harvest so he could stay the week with me and my son, Joel. As we walked down the main street to register the kids in the crèche, I broached the subject of our possible adoption to see whether she had any inkling as to whether either of us had been adopted. Perhaps she knew?

It was clear that she didn't think there was any truth in it because like me, she said that if we were adopted we would know. Besides, I was too much like our dad and she was too much like our mum to be adopted.

On my return home, I received a letter from the registrar stating that I had been adopted, with the record of my adoption in February 1968. Seeing it on paper made it official, but it still didn't seem real. But I knew I would have to ring my mum and dad and tell them I had found out. My sister had already unknowingly mentioned something, alerting them to the fact that I may have found out.

I rang. "Dad", I said, 'I've found out'.

'Found out what?' he said.

'Found out that I was adopted'.

'Oh', came the reply, and then silence. 'I think you need to come down to Leeds, and I'll tell you everything I know'.

I could hear my mum crying in the background. Why was she crying? What was all that about?

Going down to Leeds was a little bit weird, because although nothing had changed, everything in my world had: my perception of who I was, was in question. The knowledge of my being adopted didn't change my parents' and my family's view of who I was and their relationship with me or their love for me because they had always known. But it was different for me because I didn't really know who I was anymore. It was also different to some extent for my sister who didn't know about the adoption either.

It still didn't seem real, and I didn't know what to expect. I walked into the house, and my dad had the brown box out from the upstairs cupboard, the one that we were never to go into because it held all his important papers. He produced my adoption certificate. There it was, completely real, from the Leeds Juvenile Court in 1968.

There was a weird sort of silence because I didn't know what to say, but my dad said to me, 'When you were 16 I wanted to tell you, but you were in the middle of your exams and I couldn't do it to you. Then when you were 18, you were again doing exams. Then when you got married, you looked so happy I just couldn't do it. Besides, I couldn't see you as anyone else's daughter apart from mine'.

My dad wasn't comfortable being emotional in front of us, but it was clear that for him and my mum, telling me this was one of the hardest things they had ever done. They knew I could react in a number of ways. But there was a difference between them. My mum was crying and thought I might not want them anymore and might reject them or be angry with them for not telling me. I probably spent more time with my dad talking to him. He knew me and what I thought and how I did things. He was more secure in our relationship and knew I was his daughter and nothing would change that. He knew I loved him as my dad and nothing would change that.

My sister wasn't adopted. My parents had thought they would not have children, but as often happens after they adopted me, my mum became pregnant and Jillian arrived. Before me they had tried to adopt a little boy called Andrew, and he had been with them for a short time. But then Andrew's mother came back; she had changed her mind.

Small incidents that had occurred over the years began to click into place. There were Christmas cards for Andrew in the loft that I'd asked about and was told this would have been my name if I were a boy. There were the cine films of my dad with a baby wearing blue. Why had they dressed me in blue? That time with Andrew was heart-breaking. The child they thought was theirs was taken away. My auntie told me he'd come with nothing. They bought everything for him and lavished their love on him, and when he left, they gave him everything they had given him.

When we walk away from our heavenly Father, it breaks his heart. He doesn't take away what he has given us, and, as in the prodigal son story, the father gives him everything he has, his inheritance. But like the father in the story, I don't doubt for a minute that if Andrew's mother had come back with him again and changed her mind, they would have welcomed him back with open arms.

The conversation cleared up a lot of unanswered questions for me as well. I used to wonder, why did my sister have size three and four shoes and mine were eights? Why did I have blonde hair and they all had dark hair? Something I didn't really take too seriously growing up because one of my cousins had blond hair as well, and another had big feet, but nonetheless, they were questions I had considered but just never really thought deeply about.

Points to Consider

God can turn the mess that we make of our lives into really good stuff if we are willing to let him sort out our lives. We often walk away from God and don't listen to what he has to say. But he is always there to welcome us back, and he wants us to come back. It is never right to glorify what we have done in the past that is wrong, but it is right to point people to the amazing grace of God and the way that he never abandons us.

1. Write down and share with a congregation a time when you got it wrong and how God forgave you.

   Telling people difficult things can be hard because we don't know how they're going to react, and it may not be the way you want them to. I could have easily been angry with my parents or completely walked away from them. If we're going to be proclaimers of truth, sometimes it may be difficult, and people may react to the thing you have told them and personalise it against you.

   When that happens, what support networks do you have in place to help you cope?

CHAPTER 7

Not wanting to Believe

MY DAD SAID, 'I knew once you found out you would want to find out about your birth parents, and I'll tell you as much as I know. But the person to ask is Uncle Ronny, because he knows more about your family than we do'.

I think at that point, hearing it from my dad was when it hit me most and sent me into a state of denial. It was like, in some way, I was suffering a bereavement, everything that I was certain about in my family, everything I was certain about myself had been taken away. I didn't want it to be true. How could it be true? My mum and dad were my mum and dad. I didn't want or need any other mum and dad.

I went round to see Paul, who was the leader of the house group that I went to when I was a teenager, and I cried and cried and told him how I didn't want any other parents, I had my family; I loved my family; I didn't want this to be true, and I wanted it just to go away. It wasn't a choice I'd wanted to make as to whether I accepted it. It meant I had to work things out that I never thought were an issue, things I really never wanted to even consider.

I'd just given birth to my son Joel, and my love for him was so strong I couldn't work out how anyone could give a child away. If they did, I wondered how they could deal with it, because it would have been such a massive emotional wrench. I don't think I could have ever done that with Joel. I could see there was pain in everything: in my mum not being able to have children, in my birth mother having to give her child away, in my loss of certainty about things. I was torn between knowing my birth caused great pain and emotional distress for some but had brought hope and joy to others.

When you consider those in the Bible who were adopted – Moses, for instance. You can imagine the pain his mother would have felt having to give her new-born away to save his life, the pain of never being able to tell him as he grew up that she was his mother, but you can also imagine the joy and happiness he brought his adopted mother (see appendix 3).

The birth of Jesus would have brought pain and anguish to the family of Mary and Joseph. Imagine the turmoil of having their lives turned upside down, the pain and hurt that Joseph must have felt, when he found out, before he was told in a dream the truth, that his fiancé was pregnant and he wasn't the father but then finding out the joy his child would bring to the world. What happened at the end of Jesus' life brought distress and heartbreak. If you have ever watched the film *The Passion of the Christ* and followed Mary as she follows Jesus through the whole execution and death of her son, you can see the pain and sorrow the disciples and his friends went through. But then there was that joy three days later when he was resurrected. He was alive!. That same joy millions over the centuries have been able to feel by having a relationship with God made possible only because of the pain of the cross.

But I didn't want my adoption to be real! I kept telling myself it wasn't real, that I didn't want this! I just wanted it to be like it was before I found out, when I had that security.

Paul quickly reminded me that his children were adopted and no one could ever tell him they weren't his children and that's how my mum and dad must feel. I was their child, and they would never stop being my mum and dad. He then reminded me about how God had adopted me, and in the same way, I'd always be his child. He then prayed a very important prayer – although I didn't realize it at the time – that I would feel secure in my relationship with my family and in my relationship with my heavenly Father.

I talked to him about finding out about and meeting my birth parents, and he told me how it is probably something my mum and dad would expect I would want to do, because they knew me well. He said to remember that I may not like what I find out but to also remember that God had planned things before I was even born. He had it all in hand. God gave me my mum and dad for a reason: because he loves me a lot. Psalm 139:13–17 says:

> For it was you who formed my inward parts; you knit me together in my mother's womb. I praise you, for I am fearfully and wonderfully made. Wonderful are your works; that I know very well. My frame was not hidden from you, when I was being made in secret, intricately woven in the depths of the earth. Your eyes beheld my unformed substance. In your book were written all the days that were formed for me, when none of them as yet existed. How weighty to me are your thoughts, O God! How vast is the sum of them!

Also, a favourite verse of his was Romans 8:28: 'We know that in everything God works for good with those who love him, who are called according to his purpose'.

The story of God, through what Jesus did for us on the cross, is one people can shy away from and not want to accept because it's so horrific. Our sin, the wrong things that *we* have said and done and thought have separated us from God. But because Jesus loves us that much, he was willing to go through the pain of the cross no matter what the cost so that the price of our sin could be paid for and we could have our relationship with God restored.. If that doesn't get us to our knees in gratitude for his love and grace and faithfulness, nothing will.

Often we switch off mentally from trauma and pain and things we don't want to face because it's easier than facing the pain. But when we do face these situations, we have to remember that God has things in hand. Without the cross there cannot be a resurrection, without pain there cannot be healing, and without despair there cannot be hope.

God is not distant from these situations of pain; he is right there in the centre, holding our hands, guiding us through them. Often, people assume God is not there because they can't feel him, and can't see him. They have let go of his hand, but God never lets us go. It's a bit like when I used to take my children out and they didn't want to hold my hand because they wanted to be independent, so I walked close to them and held onto their hoods without them knowing. They might not have held tightly to me, but I never let go.

It is important that we ensure that the people we are preaching to know without a shadow of a doubt that God loves them, that he made them and knows everything about them. And although we might not be able to handle the situation we find ourselves in, and we might not even want to accept it because the thought of it is so painful, God is right there. It's a *fact*!

God wants us to be secure in that knowledge that he has it in control.

Being adopted by God means we are loved. As we have seen, the promises and love of God are so fantastic, they are almost unbelievable. But we can be sure that we can trust what he has told us, and as we can trust him, we should do our best to live in a way that pleases him.

Points to Consider

If we look again at Wesley's Sermon Number 9 (see appendix), that second phase of man, the man under the law is the person who sees things as they are, feels the pain of what has happened, and feels that feeling of conviction.

1. Is it possible to go from the natural man state to the redeemed man without going through the man under the law state?

2. In Isaiah 58:12, it says 'You will use the old rubble of past lives to build anew, rebuild the foundations from out of your past'. What things in your past that seem like rubble is God using in your present?

3. Devise a visual aid to show how God can rebuild broken lives.

4. Watch the film *The Passion of the Christ*. Each person in the group chooses a character from the film. What would they be feeling during the crucifixion? Share this with each other and then pray.

5. Use a clip on YouTube, such as the song 'Mary Did You Know?' from *The Passion of the Christ* or 'Perfect Love (Mary's Song)', and devise a Bible study for a small group about pain and suffering and why it happens.

CHAPTER 8

Knowing Where You Come From

IT FELT A bit strange going back home to South Shields in some ways. I felt empty inside. It felt like a bereavement, like something within me had died. My security was gone. The fact is it hadn't, but the whole emotional thing was there, and I wasn't really able to take it in and process it. In other ways, there was this massive sense of relief about why I was different.

There were people who asked whether I was angry that my mum and dad didn't tell me before, and to be honest, in my case I think my parents did the right thing. Had my sister and I known about it when we were teenagers, we would have used it against each other, because like all sisters, we used to argue. My sister and I were very similar in lots of ways, such as in our views on things, but we were very different in other ways.

But there was also this sense of people not being honest with us. Everyone in the family knew about the adoption apart from us, and it could have been seen as living a lie. However, it could be seen in two other ways: they said nothing because of their love for us, and they said nothing because they actually forgot; the adoption was so complete that the fact that I was adopted meant I was nothing other than their daughter.

I remember my dad telling me that 'blood is thicker than water' on lots of occasions and also him talking to me about how I'll probably turn out like my mother. I think he often forgot, because he couldn't see me as anything apart from his daughter. That was total adoption.

The days that followed were some of the strangest of my life. I plucked up the courage to ring Uncle Ronny. I had four uncles, all of whom were very different. Uncle Syd always made us all laugh; Uncle Sid bought us ice cream, and Uncle Alf and I used to talk at length about life, the universe, and everything.

But Uncle Ronny was the one my cousins seemed to be the most cautious about visiting, because they knew they had to behave at his house or they would be in trouble. I loved and still do love going to his house, because even when my cousins were in trouble, I would never get into trouble for the same things. He was always interested in what I was doing, and he's interested in what my children are doing. When I stayed at his house during school holidays, I was treated like one of his children.

I loved school holidays and staying at Otley and going out with my cousins. I especially loved going out with my cousin Debbie, who I always aspired to because she was going to be a nurse, and I wanted to be a doctor. When there was any danger that I might upset Uncle Ronny by doing something wrong, she would warn me, and I'm sure she always took the blame when I did do anything wrong. I always used to think Uncle Ronny knew what I was thinking, what I would do, and how I would react to things, and this might possibly be because he was aware of the nature of my birth family. When we're adopted, we still have our birth parents genes and the things that were there from the beginning in us, but we're given a new home and environment and are nurtured.

Some people can use this as an excuse as to why people are like they are – 'they have it in them'. I remember talking to a parent of one of my daughter's friends. They had adopted her and were telling me how she'll probably turn out: out of control, and end up in prison like her parents. I asked whether the husband was in prison. I knew he wasn't. I was trying to make a point. Why would the girl end up being a problem? They adopted her and are the ones who will nurture her, who will influence the formation of her character.

I heard an interesting sermon recently at the church that I attend. It was pointing out that although people in our family history may not always have been people to be proud of, that doesn't mean God doesn't redeem the situation. He used the example of Abraham's nephew Lot. Lot really messed up, had sex with his daughters who gave birth to his sons.

When my parents adopted me, yes, I came with a certain genetic makeup, and there are some similarities in my personality to my birth parents', but I can never blame my behaviour on them. We make our own decisions in life about whether we are going to do right or wrong. We can't blame it on others.

As adopted children of our heavenly Father, we are given everything we need to live a life of holiness, a life in relationship with him, but we often reject it. We can make excuses, such as, 'I can't do anything about it', or 'I was made like that', but when God adopts us, he moulds us into his likeness if only we let him.

Uncle Ronny told me my birth parents' names and how his best friend was my grandfather. He told me how I'd met them. He also told me he might be able to find my birth mother's telephone number because her friend just lived round the corner in Otley.

Within an hour I had contact numbers for a whole group of strangers who knew about me and seemed to know quite a lot about me, but they were people I didn't even know existed or wasn't sure I wanted to know.

I was told my birth mother already had a little girl when she had me and she was only 17 at that time. My birth father was in prison, and she was staying with his parents. My grandparents mentioned to my aunt and uncle that my birth mother was looking for a good home for me and asked whether they wanted me. Auntie Mary said they would have taken me if they had not already had five children of their own, but she told them she knew a couple who wanted a baby.

She knew what had happened with Andrew and that they were still struggling with losing him, and she knew how much my mum and dad wanted a baby. So they rang my mum and dad up and asked if they wanted me, and of course they did.

That very afternoon my mum packed in work, and they made arrangements with Uncle Alf to go to Otley and get me.

When they brought me home, I went first to Uncle Alf's, where my new cousins were waiting for me. My cousin Tracey, who was only 5 at the time, asked, 'Can we keep her?' Of course the answer was yes. There was no hesitation. I was now part of the Thompson family.

When we become Christians, it's important that we know we've been given a new life.

Points to Consider

1. When new Christians come to our church, do we show excitement? Do we expect to keep them? How do you go about supporting and nurturing new Christians?
2. In a group, work out what you think are the ten most important things that you need to help a new Christian with.
3. Have a debate within your group as to which is more important, nature or nurture, but use biblical examples to argue your case.

CHAPTER 9

No Hesitation

MY MUM STOPPING work to have me and my dad agreeing to the adoption without hesitation is a wonderful picture of the love of God.

If we offer ourselves to God, there is no hesitation. Does he want us? Of course he does. More than anything he wants a relationship with his creation.

Adopting me could have meant more hurt for my parents. But they were willing to risk it, willing to put themselves on the line for me. They knew love hurts because they had experienced that with Andrew, but they did it anyway. They were prepared to risk the hurt again of having a child and possibly losing me if my birth mother changed her mind.

God knows people will reject him. He knows his children will get it wrong, that they will often walk away, but he's willing to put everything on the line because he loves us and desires a relationship with us.

God is always willing to have us back. He doesn't hesitate to adopt us even though it cost him everything, it hurt, but still he gave everything for us.

I often tell the following story when I'm preaching to illustrate God's lack of hesitation towards us and his love for us. It's about a mining village, and I heard a version of it when I was a teenager, and it's stuck with me.

A community of miners lived at the top of a very steep hill. You could almost describe it as a mountain. Every day, ready for work, the miners climbed onto a bus, and the bus driver drove them down the steep, narrow road to the bottom, using the skill that only the bus driver had – he'd been doing this route for years! He would then drive back up the mountain and get the next load of miners for the next shift. At the end of each shift, he brought everyone home. Everyone knew who the driver was, although they didn't know his name. They trusted him and enjoyed the ride, and he got them where they needed to be.

But one day everything changed. The bus driver met the miners at the top of the mountain as usual. It had been snowing, and the road was treacherous. Snow was still falling, and they knew their journey would be slow. However, because they trusted the driver who always got them where they needed to go and got them there safely, they weren't worried.

As expected, he drove very slowly, but still the wheels were slipping. It was hard to see the way ahead but the bus driver kept on driving. He knew that if he went too far to the left the bus would drop down the side of the mountain and they would all die, and if he swerved to the right, the bus would crash into the side of the mountain and they would all die. So he continued on the route, never taking his eye off the road.

All seemed to be going well until they were nearly at the bottom, and the miners could see a small child starting to walk in the road in front them. They started shouting at the driver to stop, but he never flinched.

He kept his eyes on the road and kept going, and as the bus was getting closer to the child, the miners were going crazy, trying to stop the driver, but the driver kept going. They heard and felt a stomach-churning *thud!* Still the driver kept going.

Those on the bus wanted to get off and go back, but the driver couldn't stop. There were tears in his eyes, but he didn't look back. Eventually he came to a stop at the bottom of the mountain. Some of the miners ran back to try to find the child, and others yelled at him. 'Why? Why did you do it?'

He replied, 'Because if I had not have kept going, you all would have died. That was my son who died!'

God risked everything because of his love for us, and he did it without hesitation.

In a sermon I heard a number of years ago, Phil Wall, a Salvation Army evangelist, spoke about a concert that U2 did where lead singer Bono's life was threatened. They were informed that if the band performed a particular song, they were all likely to die. But they knew it was the right thing to do it. On stage, when they started to sing the particular song they had been threatened over, one of the band members manoeuvred himself in front of Bono without hesitation. He was willing to put himself in the way of the bullet.

God is willing to take the punishment for us, without hesitation, because he loves us.

For many, this story is difficult because they find it so much easier to give than receive, especially as we get older. We can handle giving our own lives for something more than we can handle someone giving their lives for us. When people went to war in the First World War, many came back with stories of their friends giving their lives for them. Survivors lived with guilt because they didn't die. They should have died but someone else had died in their place and they didn't feel deserving of such a sacrifice. Children are much more willing to receive and accept things. They love getting presents. They accept the love we give them far more readily than adults do. They trust more, and as parents we love to give and see them happy. God is the perfect Father; he loves to give us good things, but we have to receive that love like a child.

Mark 10:15 tells us, 'I tell you the truth, anyone who will not receive the kingdom of God like a little Child will never enter it'.

The sacrifice that Jesus gave he gave willingly and without hesitation; the gift of life that he has given us is something we need to accept without hesitation and receive with gratitude and love because he is our Father who wants us to be his children.

Points to Consider

1. Why do we find it difficult to accept things from others and from God?
2. There is a story about a man who was walking down the road with a heavy load on his back. The walk was long, and he was tired. Along the road came a man with a van who stopped and offered him a lift. The man, although he desperately wanted a lift, thought there was no way that the van driver could fit him and the heavy load into his van, so he declined the offer. He carried on.

   The van driver drove past him later that day. When he saw him exhausted on the side of the road, he offered him a lift again, but the man turned him down again because he didn't think that both he and his load would fit in the van.

   Finally, towards the evening, the van driver drove past again and pleaded with him to get in the van and accept the lift. The man explained that although he was very tired and was very grateful for the van driver's offer, he didn't think that the van driver would want to take him and all his baggage and he would feel bad about putting him to all that trouble.

The van driver said, 'I have spent all day trying to understand what I'd done wrong that you didn't want to get into the van with me. When I offered you a lift, it was an offer of a lift for you and everything that you are carrying'.

The man got in the van with a struggle because he still had the heavy load on his back.

The van driver said, 'Take the load off and put it in the back. Let me carry that in my van and you sit at the front with me, and I'll take you to your destination'.

This is a picture of what it can often be like for people within our churches, including ourselves. God doesn't hesitate to be there for us, to give everything for us, but we don't accept it. There are lots of things in this story that we can relate to our journey in life and how God deals with us.

How could you use this story to talk about God?

3. Try to think of situations in your church or in your life where people have tried to resolve difficult situations or cope with them by themselves, often unsuccessfully, rather than allowing God to undertake for them. Then write a similar story that may make people think about God's lack of hesitation to love us unconditionally.

4. Produce some artwork, drama or PowerPoint presentation that can help people understand that God doesn't hesitate.

5. There are lots of stories about Christians who have given their lives for others, for example, people like Maximilian Kolbe ('The Saint from Auschwitz') and theologian Dietrich Bonhoeffer. Look at the Christian history of your town or city. Were there people who didn't hesitate to give up everything for Jesus? Tertullian said, 'The blood of the martyrs is the seed of the church'. Who are the saints that your church was built on?

6. For people who are making sacrifices of their lives for Jesus and for others, look on the websites of organisations such as Barnabas Trust www.https://www.barnabasfund.org. How can you get your congregation to know what it is like to

give everything? How can you enable them to pray more effectively for our Christian brothers and sisters who are suffering persecution?

7. What does the Bible tell us about guilt and not feeling good enough? Make a list of scripture verses about this and then use them in your prayers of confession or even in prayers of intercession.

CHAPTER 10

Be My Child

GOD DOESN'T ASK anything of us except for us to be his children.

All I came with was a nappy. The story went that when I got to my mum and dad's house I had nothing, so I had to wear my cousin's nightie and sleep in a drawer until my grandmother could go out the following day and buy all the things a new-born needs and more. I'd always been told I'd slept in a drawer and wore my cousin's nightie, so hearing this did answer a question I'd always wondered about: Didn't they have nine months to sort out getting me some clothes and a cot?

When we come to God, we can come with just ourselves and nothing else. He doesn't ask anything more. My mum and dad didn't ask for me to come with a wardrobe full of clothes or a whole load of baby equipment or toys. From that point I was their daughter, and they would give me all that I needed and more. I was given a new home, a new way of living, a new life.

Many people have this false idea that in order to be accepted by God, in order for him to be able to love them, in order for them to have him become their father, they need to come in a certain way, wear the right clothes, do things in a certain way. But God wants us to come as we are; he will change us.

As we grow closer to him, the more we will be like him, but when we first become Christians, we are not expected to be some sort of super saint. When you look in the Bible at the unlikely people that

Jesus called, the unlikely people he associated with, then you can see that what God wants is us as we are, and even the greats in the bible such as Peter messed up big time in his life, and the disciples constantly got it wrong. He loves us just as we are; we're a work in progress, not the finished article.

When I was adopted, my mum and dad bought me new clothes and changed my physical situation, but I was in no way the perfect daughter. I wasn't always well behaved. I got things wrong and didn't always do as I was told. I had temper tantrums, let them down, and did things I shouldn't, but because I was their daughter they guided me, corrected me, nurtured me, and moulded me. They didn't change my personality, the person I was, and they positively encouraged that. I know that no matter how much they tried, I was never going to be interested in the pretty sparkly dresses and makeup that my sister was into, but they did begin to teach me how to be their daughter and how to be a member of the family. I was given a new identity, and I took on the mannerism of my dad and the behaviours of both parents, but I was still me.

In the same way that we become more like Jesus as we walk with him (even though he only asks that we come as we are), God made us special and individual, unique and it's something he sees as good because he looked at his creation and said, 'It is good' (Genesis 1:31). He loves us as we are; he will do the rest.

Being adopted by God means we are accepted into his family, and this brings lots of blessings. Being adopted by God means he will care for us. An adoptive father in New Testament times and the Roman empire was also granted the full rights and responsibilities of a natural father – he had complete authority over the adopted son and the legal role of caregiver.

With full, loving authority over us, God has accepted his responsibility to care for us and he also has the right, and desire, to correct us when we are wrong and to discipline us when we step out of line.

Our Father God is infinitely patient, wise, and loving, and the Bible tells us that the fact that God *does* discipline us is proof in itself that we have been adopted into his family. (Proverbs 3.11-12)

I cannot remember my dad shouting at me or losing his temper with me, although I'm sure he must have, but he had a far worse way of dealing with our misbehaviour. I never wanted to let him down or upset him. You knew when he was disappointed because he went quiet, and you just longed for 'the talk' that always happened later on after you had stewed for a while. That feeling of letting him down and disappointing him hurt far more than a slap or some other physical punishment. I often wished that he would just do that and get it over with.

My dad knew what would be most effective with me, and he cared about me enough to correct and discipline me when I needed it, but the discipline worked because of the relationship that I had with my dad. The way he corrected me was only effective because I loved him so much and he loved me.

My mum and dad were given the new job of protecting me. I didn't have a responsibility to defend them or make sure that they were safe, I came as a helpless little baby with nothing and they expected to do that for me as a child. Most parents will do anything to protect their children, and the thing that upsets me more than anything as a parent is seeing my children upset, especially when something has happened where you know there has been an injustice. Both of my children have disabilities, so throughout their childhood I have constantly had to fight battles to protect them and to ensure they get the right treatment. I protect them as much as I can from things that are going to hurt. I don't ask anything of my children. I expect to do this for them because they are my children and I am their mother and that's my job.

As a teenager I was always arguing with my mum. I was always very independent and gave the impression that I was confident. But one day has always stayed with me. I was in the sixth form, and I was one of the leaders of the Christian Union, the head of sixth form seemed to have made it his mission to make life as uncomfortable as possible for those who professed a faith. Looking back now he probably strengthened the faith of many young people within the school by the way he openly made sarcastic comments about the Christians.

At the end of the first term he told me there was no point in my staying on at school because I wasn't going to pass any exams and I'd be better off getting a job. My mum and dad knew how hard I worked for my O levels and how much the study that I was doing meant to me. I'd gone home and was in my room crying. Usually my mum wouldn't come upstairs, but on this occasion she came in and saw me crying. I was heartbroken. She calmed me down and hugged me.

The next day she went down to the school and sorted it out. I've no idea what she said, but I remember that when I got my degree, she went straight back to that teacher and showed him the certificate. I didn't ask her to do any of that. She did that because she was my protector and my defender. It was what she did because she was my mother.

Because they were my parents, they were given the new role of teaching me. They didn't know what it would be like to teach me anything how could they? All children learn in different ways, and the big mistake that we as teachers make is that we try to teach children, and adults as well, to learn in a particular way. They are all individuals and all come with different gifts, backgrounds, ways of doing things, and understanding. We come to God as we are, and he teaches us in the way that is best for us. Both of my children learn in very different ways, and my way of learning is very different from theirs.

My dad was not academic in any way, but he was always very practical and taught me how to do things like change a plug and a light bulb, know how to fix things, change the tyre of my car, put shelves together, etc. Most of what he taught me has been more use to me than any of the books that I've read.

He also taught me how to deal with failure. He knew I didn't handle that well. When I was learning to swim, in order to get a badge I had to jump off a high diving board. I was up there for what seemed hours and hours and I cried because I didn't want to do it. I couldn't. I was scared to jump, and in the end I just didn't do it. I gave up. They could have given me the badge anyway, but my dad made sure I didn't get it and made me keep trying until I did. He knew I was upset and disappointed because my cousin Michaela, who was the same age as me, did jump and got her badge. But it was important that I learned that lesson, and he made sure I did. He won the same battle with my daughter twenty years later when she locked herself in the toilets having been disqualified in a swimming race!

My dad would help me to put things right when I got things wrong and would stand by me and support me even when he knew I was wrong. He didn't walk away from me. My dad accepted me as I was. His job was to teach me, and that's what he did.

God teaches us, not always in the way that we want but in the way that is best for us as individuals. If we just allow him to, if we come as ourselves, be teachable, he can do it.

And lastly, their new job was to provide for me. This provision was all one sided and what they desired to do for me. I came with nothing. I wasn't expected to provide anything. God wants to provide for us, and when he adopts us, he will provide all that we need. Not necessarily what we want but what we need because that is his nature.

Points to Consider

1. On a large sheet of paper, write the words WHO AM I? And then write all the words and things that you think about yourself and what describes who you are. How does that compare to who God says you are in God's love letter in the first chapter?

2. Ask another two or three people to write down who they think you are and words that describe you. What does this tell you? What action should to take as a result?

3. Some people will get things wrong in church and with their relationships with God, and the easiest thing to do is walk away. What would you say to someone who said, 'I am not good enough'? What would be your three points if you were writing a sermon about it?

4. John Wesley and the early Methodists were big into accountability and discipline. Are we too scared as preachers to actually say that certain things are right or wrong because of trying to not upset people?

5. Put together some of your own experiences and other people's stories about how God has provided for you. Is there a way of sharing these stories to encourage others? Could you use a Facebook page or a newsletter?

6. Isaiah 58:11 says, 'The Lord will guide you always he will satisfy your needs'. Produce a short talk for a small group of people such as a home group or ladies meeting or youth group based on this verse. Keep it to three minutes! What would you say?

7. What should our response be to our own failure as Christians?

8. How can the church help those who feel they have failed?

9. People learn in various ways. Preaching a sermon is limited as a teaching method because you need a particular style of learning to benefit from it. In a group, look at different ways people learn and then plan a service together where different teaching styles are used in different parts of the service.

CHAPTER 11

A New Name

THE ONLY THING I had which belonged to me when I went to my new parents was my name, JoAnne. When I asked my mum why she didn't change my name, she said, 'It was the only thing that your birth mother gave you, so we decided that you should keep it'.

When we come to God, when we become Christians, we don't lose our personality, the thing that makes us *us*, because God gave us our own personality. He knows us by name. But what he does do is give us a new name. I wasn't known as JoAnne Cross or JoAnne Paley from the minute that I went to live with my mum and dad. I was given the new name of Thompson, my family name, but I kept the name I was born with, JoAnne, which means 'God is gracious', and he most certainly was!

My adoption took place a year later. I understand that my family were very protective about me and ensured that no one from my birth family knew where I lived because of the experience with Andrew, but after the year passed, which was the legal limit for taking me back, my birth mother signed the papers, and on 22 February 1968 I officially became JoAnne Thompson. It tells me on my adoption certificate that my father is Jack Thompson, a Joiner, and my mother, Doreen Thompson, is his wife. There are no other names on that certificate.

Christians are adopted as sons and daughters into God's family. Paul uses the term 'adopted as sons' to write to the believers in Rome, where they would have understood this in a specific context. Under Roman law, if you were an adopted son, you had identical legal rights to a son born naturally in the family. An adopted son had the right to the family name of the person who adopted him and the right to an inheritance of the father's property. The adopted son also had the right to the father's citizenship of the Empire. We also obtained a new citizenship when our Father adopted us and we become citizens of heaven.

In British law adopted children do not have any rights to an inheritance from their birth parents but have the same rights as any other child to an inheritance form their adopted parents.

For Christians, this means we have been given the name of Christ and have the right to be called Christians. Our inheritance is nothing less than the property of our heavenly Father – all the spiritual riches that are in Christ, both in the present life and in our life to come.

Three days later I was taken to the local church, and my mum, dad, and family came to celebrate my baptism. The first thing they did for me was to thank God for me, confirm my name, dedicate my life to God, and make promises on my behalf that I would follow Jesus.

Points to Consider

1. Why is a name important?
2. Look at the meaning of your name. Devise a children's talk about the importance of names. Perhaps it could be one devised for Advent, and the naming of Jesus ('his name shall be called Immanuel' Matthew 1:23). Or could it be about the different names of Jesus and what they mean?
3. Write down as many names for God the Father/Son and Holy Spirit as you can from the Bible. What do they mean?

4. In the Old Testament there are children that are named pretty awful names based on how their parents saw them or the circumstances of their birth. All children are a gift from God, and made in the image of God. He rejoices in the birth of every child and knows each by name. But he made us all unique and individual and with a different role to play.

Write a prayer of thanks based on God's goodness that could be used in a thanksgiving/dedication service for a child. (Would you change the prayer if the child had a disability or medical condition?)

CHAPTER 12

Security

A DAY OR two passed, after speaking to my parents about the adoption and I plucked up the courage to ring my natural grandfather, Norman. Uncle Ronny assured me that he was a really nice man and I was like him. He also told me that Norman would like to meet me. I had mixed feelings about hearing that I was like him. I never had a grandfather because my granddad Thompson died before I was born, but I was part of a family where my granddad featured in a lot of things and my cousins talked about him. I knew for instance that he was involved in moulding the swan at the swan hotel in Harrogate because every time we went past, it was pointed out to me, I knew stories about my granddad giving the grandchildren money on a Sunday afternoon on his way to the club. I was told by my grandma how much he would have loved me and my sister and he was in that sense part of who I was and my upbringing. To be told I was like a different granddad was a little strange.

I agreed to meet him on the same day I spoke to my birth mother on the phone for the first time and agreed to meet her in Leeds.

Meeting Norman for the first time was actually like meeting an old friend. I had seen him before at a family party and had been introduced to him and his wife. At the time I had no idea this party had caused a lot of worry for a lot of people. I was totally oblivious to it all because I loved to go to family parties and be with my cousins.

Being introduced to a whole load of old people I was told were friends or relatives, who told you how much you had grown since they last saw you was just something that we all had to endure.

On this occasion, though, I could remember but could never understand why they were so keen for me and not my sister, Jillian, to be introduced to this particular old couple. I didn't think it was very fair because I wanted to be dancing with my cousins and not mixing with old people, but as the eldest, I just assumed it was to do with that.

But that all became clear when I met Norman. He got out a big scrapbook, which was full of pictures of me from the *Yorkshire Evening Post* and my swimming achievements, school photos, and things about me. They had watched me grow up but could never reveal who they were.

During my visit my birth father turned up drunk, and I was introduced to a young man who was my half-brother, who was a bit younger than me. He had never been aware of my existence and didn't know I would be there. He came in, and my birth father immediately introduced me: 'Jonathan, this is your sister'. The colour drained from his face.

That day I met a whole bunch of the Paley family, all of whom knew who I was – but of course I hadn't a clue who they were. I can't say it was a comfortable experience, because I was meeting a whole bunch of strangers, and it was like being in some sort of weird dream that I thought I might eventually wake up from.

The next meeting was with my birth mother at a MacDonald's in Leeds, and she was very keen to tell me what had happened and to be clear that she expected nothing of me. She understood that I had a different family but was keen to find out about me and the sort of things I did.

I showed her pictures of Joel and my family. What struck me was her honesty about the whole situation. She had obviously been living with a lot of guilt, and her giving me up for adoption had been done with nothing other than love, care, and concern for me and the welfare of her other daughter.

At its heart there were a lot of tears and heartache, but on the other hand, she told me, 'If abortion had been legal, you would have been down the plug hole'.

I'm told I should be emotionally scarred by this, but actually, for me I was even clearer that God had a plan and purpose for my life. Abortion was made legal later on in the year that I was born, so this was something that I saw as a blessing that God had control of my life right then, even before I was born, and that there was something important in this.

Given the number of children that are aborted nowadays, I can't imagine why anyone would ever hold a grudge against their natural parents for giving them up for adoption rather than having them aborted. I'm grateful for the gift of life that I was given, and I know my mum and dad were grateful for the gift of a child that my birth mother gave to them.

As a mother I can't imagine ever being able to give my child away and being able to live with the pain of that, but if it was a choice of whether my child lived or died, I would hope that I would choose life for my child. It seems to me that women who gave their children up for adoption were doing it in the best interests of the children in those days, out of love for them – perhaps even more so nowadays, and to be adopted is a blessing, not a curse. It means you were loved.

Many people still see adoption as something shameful, especially in some African countries where children are treated badly if they have been adopted. But adoption means someone loved you enough to give you to people who could care for you, and you were loved by the people who adopted you because they chose you. You were never an accident, you were wanted and loved and are privileged.

I've heard many people who are adopted talking about how they didn't have a very good family and didn't get on with their parents. I think this is often more to do with an excuse and their own insecurity than reality. Most of my friends growing up had issues with their parents as do my own children with me, and they were not adopted. The fact that you don't always get on with your parents is sometimes probably a healthy sign that you are accepted and belong.

When I think of my own daughter, Laura, and the fact that she is unlikely to have children naturally because of her condition, it makes me realize there certainly is the 'fingerprint of God' on our lives. Laura has no problems with the idea of adoption and sees this as something quite normal because I was adopted. Even for that I can see God was working,

My niece and nephew were also very much affected by the fact that they have father figures who took on the role of their dad but are not their biological fathers. For my nephew especially, my being adopted and the way that was accepted within the family helped him in his life. The most stable male in his life was my dad, and he was able to see parenting as more than a biological thing. My niece also recognises that her dad is the one who has loved and nurtured her and who she calls dad but isn't her biological father. They were loved and had security in knowing that the men they called dad were very much their fathers.

There was an experiment done with children in a school playground which had a high fence around it. The teacher stayed in the playground, and the children were happy to play and run about. Then they put the same children in the playground after removing the fences, and the children lost their confidence despite the fact that the teacher was there. They lost their freedom and bunched up near the door. Their sense of security was in the fence, not in the fact that the teacher was there.

When we I found out about the adoption, it was like the fence was taken away. The things that held me together were taken away, but the important thing to do was to stay close to the Father. If we stay close to and in hearing distance of the Father, we remain in a place of safety and security.

God gave me a family I was made to feel part of, a very secure family, with parents who saw me as nothing but their own and an extended family who loved me and made sure I was accepted.

I could only feel gratitude to my birth mother for what she did. She was in a position where the best she could do for me was to give me to people who would give me a good home and I am so very grateful that she did.

▨ Points to Consider

1. What are things in your life upon which you base your security?

2. Many people leave the church because their security is built on the church rather than God. It's built around people rather than God. When things go wrong in the church – which they do because it's full of imperfect people – people walk away from the church and God because of it. How can we change the way we do church and preach to help people understand that our faith and security has to be in our relationship with God and not the church?

3. In twos visit people who, over the last three years have left the church or no longer come on a regular basis. Find out why. Do a report for your church council and suggest ways you could help those who have been visited to be included and to know that it's about God, not the church.

4. Something that people often feel, both in the church and as adopted children, is the feeling of rejection and because of this they often feel insecure. When this happens it can be a very lonely place to be. Do you meet regularly with other Christians outside of your fellowship to pray and support each other? As a preacher there will be times when God tells you to preach something or do something that people will not like. It is vital that we ensure that we all have a support network in our Christian lives. Who are the people you meet with to pray and be accountable to? Who are the people you know you can turn to? What are the scriptures that you turn to when you are feeling like this?

5. Look up organisations, such as the Inspire Network (www. InspireMovement.org) or places where people are able to

encourage you (e.g., the Northumbria Community (www. northumbriacommunity.org). Make sure you're not alone; we were built for relationships. (There are lots of other Christian groups. Look them up and enable your congregation to have access to them as well.)

6. What songs and hymns could you use in a service when talking about the security that we find in our Father God?

7. In the hymn 'Blessed Assurance', what did the writer mean when she talked of blessed assurance?

As Methodists, we're supposed to be big into 'assurance of sins forgiven', but many in our churches are often insecure about their faith and unsure whether they really are loved by God. Write a talk or sermon on assurance. Do you have that assurance yourself?

CHAPTER 13

Making Sense of It— Don't Look Back

AFTER THE INITIAL meeting of various members of my birth family, I set to work on the family trees to try to put my birth in some sort of context. But really, it was like doing someone else's family tree because I was very much part of the Thompson clan. That was my family and my heritage and my history.

In our Christian lives, it's sometimes tempting to go back to things that happened before you became a Christian. It's good to see where you've come from and how amazing and gracious God is in adopting us as his children, but it is never good to dwell on it too much. Adoption is about a new future and to go back to the past doesn't always help us to move forward and grow in our faith.

For a good example of the dangers of looking back read the story of Lot's wife in Genesis chapter 19.

There was another time when I agreed to meet up with my birth father, but again, he had to be drunk to meet me and had no idea how to act towards me. His treatment of my birth mother and the way he spoke to her was derogatory towards women and so alien to the way my mum and dad brought me up to respect others that I found it too difficult to cope with.

The devil will constantly challenge us about whether it really did happen: Are you really a child of God? Wouldn't you rather be doing this? This is what you could have been doing.

I'm part of a family that has a strong moral code and are very protective and supportive of each other. My dad would have never allowed me to badmouth others or to swear, so when confronted with this, would I rather be part of the past? No. I had within me something that made me like my family. I was wholly part of them, and they were wholly part of me, and some things were just not acceptable.

Our adoption by God also changes our relationship with everybody – both Christians and non-Christians. Our relationship to everyone else who has been adopted by God is changed, and no matter what the distance is between us – whether they live near or far, or whether they are alive today or have already died, they are all our brothers and sisters.

Our relationship with non-believers has also changed; they are still dead in their sins, and we are no longer part of what they are about. We have different interests from them now.

Questions to Consider

1. Is it ever right to be one of the crowd and join in the things that you did before you became a Christian?
2. Where do you draw the line with 'being in the world but not of the world' (Romans 12:2)? Try to think of different situations where this could apply. How would you encourage your congregation to think about these issues?
3. Is your life distinctive because of your relationship with God?

CHAPTER 14

Growing Up

AS WE GROW in our Christian lives, we can stay at the stage of adoption and never move forward – have the new clothes and the new name but that's it. It's only by developing a personal relationship with God as Father and having an intimacy with him that you start to grow.

In Proverbs 3:7, we are to write God's words on the tablet of our hearts. There is a difference between getting them in your head and writing them on your heart. By writing them on your heart, you can more easily walk in the truth that they contain.

'I have hidden your word in my heart that I might not sin against you' (Psalm 119:11).

Because of the laws in Deuteronomy, Jewish men have the words of God written on a little scrolls in a tefillin, which is strapped to their heads in prayer and on their arms, pointing to their hearts. It is also written on their doorpost in the mezuzah. They are reminded that the word of God is something that needs to be at the very heart of you as well as in your head. The more time you spend with God, the closer you become to him, the more your relationship develops, the more you can hear and understand what he says and why he says it, and the more you can respond to him.

Spending time with our Father God is critical, and when you do spend time with him and know him in that way, why would you ever want to be part of the way you were before you became a Christian?

I used to spend time with my dad a lot when I was young. He used to take me for early morning swimming training (I hated the early morning training) but the time that I had with my dad during those journeys to and from swimming at 5 a.m. were precious.

It was there that he imparted his wisdom to me: 'Always remember that men are different from women'. 'The best thing to do is to keep your mouth shut'. 'I'm not telling you what to do, but if I were you, I would ...'

I knew how my dad thought. I knew what upset him, I knew when I'd upset him, and I knew when he was proud of me. Although he never used to be very emotional, you always knew if something was wrong and he always knew when something had upset me even if I tried to hide it. He knew me and I knew him.

I remember on the night that he died wanting to cry and not wanting to do the things I knew I must do as his daughter. Even though he was gasping for breath, he tried to make me smile and laugh. There were things he told me to do but not my sister and mother, because he knew they would be too difficult for them to do. But somehow he knew I would be able to do the things he asked.

He also knew I wouldn't be able to cope with seeing him die, and it wasn't until after that I realized what he had done. He sent me to the shops for some Lucozade (an energy drink). If I'd have thought about it I would have known that there was no way that he would be able to drink it. He died while I was out, a last loving act to his daughter that he knew so well.

God wants to spend time with us because he is our Father, and we should want to spend time with him. As a child I loved spending time with my dad and listening to him. These were the times when he would tell us the important things for our lives. It's so important to spend time with God finding out what he wants us to do, but more importantly, just spending time with him getting to know him and just being loved by him.

Being adopted by God means many relationships will change. It means we become the children of the Living God. We have a new relationship with God – through believing in what Jesus Christ has done for us, God the condemning Judge, who should punish every sin we have ever committed according to the just and perfect law, has instead become our loving Father who forgives us.

God is no longer far off and unapproachable but is near and easily accessible; we can come to him whenever we want. The Bible tells us that God *wants* us to come to him, he longs for us to spend time with him, to talk with him about everything that is happening in our lives – our Father in heaven wants to listen to us and care for us.

Being adopted by God changes our relationship with him entirely and affects all three Members of the Trinity: with God the Father – he is no longer the Judge who must condemn us for our wrongdoings but is our loving Father.

My dad never condemned me in any way. There were times that he could have, things I did as a child that I wasn't very proud of. He was more often than not telling people about something good I'd done or what the grandchildren had done. He was proud of us and would encourage us to try again in a different way and not give up if we failed. Even in failure he didn't give up on us. He helped us cope with failure and was proud of the way we handled it and moved on.

When God adopts us, he wants us to come back to him, have the relationship restored so that we can move on.

With God the Son, not only is he our Lord and Saviour, he also becomes our Brother.

With God the Holy Spirit, he not only calls us and sanctifies us, he becomes the Spirit of adoption within us. He witnesses to our own spirit within us that we are a child of God. The Holy Spirit becomes our guarantee and our Father's initial down-payment of the divine inheritance we will receive and a seal upon our hearts that we belong to God. It is through the Holy Spirit that we can cry out to God, 'Abba, Father'.

Questions to Consider

1. How much time do you spend developing your relationship with God? If you don't spend time talking to him, reading scripture, getting to know him, it's very difficult then to find your security in a person you don't really know. Look at the amount of time and energy you put into other things including church, may be you could make a timetable of what you do in a week and then look at where you fit God into that.

2. As a preacher, it is important to spend time with God listening to him, studying his word. We have an awesome responsibility when we preach, and it should never be taken lightly. What are you doing to ensure that you are reading his word? Do you have Bible reading notes, or online daily Bible studies? Do you listen to his word on CDs or podcasts? Do you read or regularly make sure you are somewhere where you are spiritually fed and have space to hear God?

3. If prayer is not our number one priority, we cannot expect to build a relationship with God and hear what he is saying to us. What is your prayer life like? Is prayer a priority?

4. Intentionally put things in place so that you know that there are times when you can spend time just enjoying God your Father. For example, do you have a worship CD in your car? Can you rearrange your life so that there is a certain time of the day or week when you just spend time with God? What other possibilities can you think of?

5. How do you cope with failure or not getting something right?

6. Using scripture, how can you help others to do this?

7. God is a God of justice as well as a God of mercy and forgiveness. How can you illustrate this to a congregation?

CHAPTER 15

What a Future!

BEING ADOPTED MEANS you have a legally secure future. Your future was uncertain, but because a couple chose you as their child, they went to court to put their case before a judge that you should be their child for the rest of your life. They signed a legal document to that effect.

Part of being anyone's child, whether naturally or through adoption, is that there is an inheritance. One of the things about adoption from the parents' perspective is that they get to choose their heirs.

God chose his heirs:

James 2:5 says, 'Did not God choose the poor of this world to be rich in faith and heirs of the kingdom which he promised to those who love him?'

In John 15:16, we read, 'You did not choose me but I chose you ...'

It's unfortunate that verses like John 15:16 ('You did not choose me, but I chose you and appointed you so that you might go and bear fruit – fruit that will last – and so that whatever you ask in my name the Father will give you'; NIV) have been at the centre of so much controversy over the centuries. While Christians are reading this sort of thing and arguing about predestination, they're missing the point of this verse. God chose you; he wants to adopt you and be your Father. This is an incredible gift from him. You have been picked special. Rejoice over this truth.

'The Holy Spirit is called the 'spirit of adoption' because he is the witness to us of the free benevolence of God with which God the Father has embraced us in his beloved only-begotten Son to become a Father to us; and he encourages us to have trust in prayer. In fact, he supplies the very words so that we may fearlessly cry, 'Abba, Father!'[2]

Romans 8:15 says, 'For you did not receive the spirit of slavery to fall back into fear, but you have received the Spirit of children of God, and if children, then heirs – heirs of God and fellow heirs with Christ, provided we suffer with him in order that we may also be glorified with him'.

Having met my birth parents and birth family, it became clearer to me where I belonged. Yes, there were similarities between me and my birth family, but my adopted family had made me their own. My security and identity were in the parents that I knew and I know loved me; they were the ones who would always be by my side when I was ill, and even as an adult my mother was the first one by my side when I've had an operation, or when my children have been ill. When I've needed help they were there. As things in my life as an adult changed and things often got hard to deal with, it was always my mum and dad I would turn to because I knew they would be there. When one of my best friends suddenly died, it was my mum that I rang. There was nothing she could say or do, but she was listening. With my dad who I would ring, often it was things that he couldn't fix, but he wouldn't tell me what I had to do although I would get the 'I am not telling you what you have to do, but if I were you, I would …' lecture. But he would never get involved in the decisions we made. Those were ours to make, our choice, and then he would always support us whatever decision we made whether he agreed with it or not.

Ringing him was often just about hearing his voice and hearing him say, 'Well, there's nothing you can do about it, so you'll just have to get on with it'. It was the reassurance I needed.

---

[2] Institutes of the Christian Religion 3.1.3.

God gives us a new life and future, and as we grow in maturity in our faith, it is even more vital that we carry on listening, that we grow closer. After all, we're going to spend eternity with him. We have this wonderful privilege of being allowed the parent-child relationship with God himself, and this is the feature of Christianity that marks us out from any other religion – the personal relationship we have with a loving God.

Since my dad died four years ago, I have found myself ringing up his mobile just for reassurance of hearing his voice, and when he says, 'See ye later', it reminds me of that truth that we will see each other later. On the night he died, he kept saying to everyone as they came into his room, 'Thanks for everything; see ye later'.

As adopted children of God, we have that relationship with our father now on earth, but we also have that promise and that security that we will spend eternity with our heavenly Father because we are his children and he has signed the papers with the blood of his Son.

1 John 3:1–2 tells us, 'See how very much our Father loves us, for he calls us his children, and that is what we are! But the people who belong to this world don't recognise that we are God's children because they don't know him. Dear friends, we are already God's children, but he has not yet shown us what we will be like when Christ appears. But we do know that we will be like him, for we will see him as he really is'.

In Psalm 23, we read, 'The Lord is my shepherd; you are with me'.

The security of God being with us is what people need when life feels uncertain or unsteady. The knowledge that he is there even when we can't see him. I always knew when my dad was around because of the aftershave he used, and when he had hair when we were little, the Cossack hairspray smell was reassuring. He had a particular whistle that he used for the dog, and when we couldn't see my dad we always knew he was there when we heard his whistle.

With God we need to ensure that we stay so close to him that we are closer than the air we breathe.

Points to Consider

1. Use Psalm 23 as the basis for a service. What things could you use to illustrate us staying close? Use the psalm in every aspect of the service – in the hymns, prayers, children's talk, and sermon.
2. Write a short, ten-minute sermon for a funeral based on Psalm 23 and God being with us.

CHAPTER 16

The Joy and the Pain in Being Part of a Family

ANOTHER TWENTY OR so years have now passed since I found out about the adoption, and I have kept in touch with my birth family through Christmas cards and occasional letters. But it has always been something that I am aware of but not really something I've spent a lot of time thinking about. It's all very interesting, and I know in my head that I was adopted and that I came from a different background and family, but my life has been lived as the daughter of my mum and dad. I have shared the joys and pains of being part of my adoptive family, and when my dad died four years ago, when I preached at his funeral, when I said my final farewell, I knew the pain that I had was not the pain that I had for a stranger it was the pain of separation from my dad, I was his daughter.

Adoption into God's family will mean pain like there is in every family, pain in our church families, sometimes there may be rejection, misunderstandings, falling out, people leaving or dying, and the church sometimes not being the best that it can or should be.

It's important that people always remember the church isn't God's 'fault'; whatever happens within our church families, it doesn't make

God's love for us and the security that we have in him as our Father and his love for us any less.

We know we are part of God's family, which is massive, and that the church is such that we can belong to different groups, but we still have God as our Father. He is constant, he never changes, and his nature never changes, despite us changing and often getting things wrong.

There were times that my family fell out with each other and often thought it was for a good reason, and there was one occasion where this happened big time. I later found out it was about me knowing about my adoption. My mum and dad and auntie all fell out over whether I should be told. My mum and dad had made their decision, but others thought they were wrong. The motives behind the fallout were out of trying to do the right thing and out of their love for me, but what that actually caused was sadness, heartache, and the loss of friendship. When families fall out to the extent that they won't even speak to each other, everyone loses. A loving intention becomes something that is far from motivated by care and love.

In the church this is so common, and it destroys what God is doing. There are ways that God tells us to resolve issues in the Bible if only we will look at them and implement his advice. What we think is the loving thing to do is not always right. My mum and dad decided the best way for me and knew what was right for me, for others it may not have been the way that they would have done it, but my parents knew me best and know what is right, just as our Heavenly Father knows us best and knows what is right even if we don't agree with him.

God knows each of us better than anyone else, he knows us and as churches we need to submit to his will totally and do as he asks even when we can't see it ourselves. As churches we should be united as family supporting each other building each other up as family even if we don't always agree with each other.

Church meetings can be places where we pull each other down rather than build each other up and where we inflict pain and hurt on each other. God calls us to love each other, to build each other up in his family as his children, but often we are like children who want to hang onto our toys and not share. We are like children who throw a tantrum if we can't get our own way, or stamp our feet until someone gives in. If we are serious about wanting to be part of a family, part of God's family, we have to start to let go of things that we think are precious to us but really are not in terms of our relationship to God. If things are right God will bless them.

What is right is what God says and what he says is, 'Love each other' (John 13:34–35), but also he says, 'Love me with all your hearts' (Matthew 22:37).

Being part of God's family means we are at home, and home should be a place of security.

'See how these Christians love each other' (Tertullian)

Questions to Consider

Home is a place in all this world where hearts are sure of each other. It is the place of confidence. It is the place where we tear off that mask of guarded and suspicious coldness which the world forces us to wear in self defence, and where we pour out the unreserved communications of full and confiding hearts. It's the spot where expressions of tenderness gush out without sensation of awkwardness and without any dread of ridicule.

—Frederick W Robertson

1. How far does this definition of home reflect what your church is like?
2. God gave us the gospel so we could become children of God. The Bible contains many examples of adoptive relationships. What makes us family is not our blood but our common bond and relationship. How far can your church be defined as God's family?
3. What makes your church a family?

CHAPTER 17

Don't Live as an Orphan

MANY CHRISTIAN BOOKS on adoption start from the point of us all being orphans. In biblical terms an orphan was one who was without a father. Even those who physically are not orphans live their spiritual lives as though they are without a father.

Many people in today's society believe themselves to be unseen, unwanted, and unloved, but by God's grace they don't have to stay there. It's important to remember that it is the love of the Father that matters.

If you were to put your ear to the ground of modern culture today ,you would hear the agonising cries of an orphan heart. Doesn't anyone notice me? See me? Value me? Want me? Is there anywhere for me to belong? But God is constantly waiting with his arms wide open to say 'You're my child and I delight in you' (Zephaniah 3:17).

Orphans have never known the feeling of truly being a son or daughter, of being loved, of being cheered on in the way that God affirmed his son in Matthew 13 16–17 at his baptism.

One of the things that came out of the exposure of the state of Romanian orphanages to the world a number of years ago was the incredible impact that the lack of love from a parent and the constant reinforcement of worthlessness had on the children who had been abandoned in these orphanages. Lack of love stunted their physical growth, extreme stress caused a growth hormone deficiency, and those going in to see the orphans were advised not to touch them or show affection in any way because the orphans were unable to cope with someone showing them love and affection and then walking away. It was likely to cause them to beat themselves up and hit their heads against the ground because they couldn't cope with the rejection.

The cry of the orphan is, 'Won't someone see anything remotely worthwhile in me?' And all the time God says, 'I do. I really do!' Which is something people in our world need to know big time. Christians who are living in this way feeling unloved, have not grasped or accepted that God is their Father, and are still living as 'orphans'.

Questions to Consider

1. Do you really know God loves you? Do you know it in your heart as well as your head?
2. Are you living a life that shows others how much he loves you and how much he loves them?

CHAPTER 18

Set Free to Be

ONE OF MY close friends, who was adopted as an older child of eight, told me of the feeling of freedom that she found when she was adopted and when she realized she didn't have to do anything to earn the love of her parents. She had been in a number of foster placements and had often pushed them to the limits with her behaviour, but there was one couple she really wanted to stay with. This couple, who eventually adopted her, lived in a big house and had lots of money, which was how she perceived it, and materially she had things that she had only have ever dreamed about. She tried as much as she could to make them like her. She would try to do as much of the housework as she possibly could without being asked; she would make sure she was in her room straight after school to stay out of the way and not bother them; she would spend her pocket money on buying gifts for them; and she would try to be whatever she thought they wanted her to be.

This was not something the parents wanted; they wanted her to be their child not because they wanted a servant or a slave. They wanted to have a relationship with her. They wanted her to be their daughter, the person God had made her to be.

Often we try to work our way into God's favour by what we do instead of accepting his love and grace. God wants to give us freedom, not bondage. If you have been redeemed by God's work, you have nothing to prove. Eternally we have been completely proven by God.

People who have this idea of God where they are there just to serve have got it wrong. 'That's what angels do; our job is to serve'.[3]

He made humans for relationships, and we serve because we love and because he loved us (1 John 4:19). They think that their worth hinges on the value of their work.

Slaves constantly live in fear of not knowing enough, not doing enough, not ever measuring up; it's bondage and it's exhausting. Slaves are so committed to their rules and timetables that they end up ostracising the very people they are called to reach. They forget that it is about the grace of God.

My friend was eventually adopted, but it was only when she realized that the love of her new parents didn't depend on what she did, that she had freedom to be herself and freedom to be their daughter and not a servant or a slave.

The Reformation and the things around Martin Luther and his ninety-five theses on 'the Power and Efficacy of Indulgencies' in 1517 when he nailed them to the door of the church in Whittenburg was about freedom from the bondage of doing good works to get into heaven. People were slaves to human performance, and they were trying to earn or buy God's love and favour instead of understanding that it was about the grace of God.

Ephesians 2:8–9 tells us, 'It is by grace that you have been saved through faith – and this is not from yourselves, it is the gift of God – not by works so that no one can boast'.

If we go back to the story of the prodigal son, there is a place for productivity, for glorifying God with hard work, but what the older son and the younger son had to understand before they could really live as sons was that the father's love was not based on good deeds.

It's interesting when we look at Jesus' baptism, the Spirit of God comes on Jesus, as God says in Luke 3:22, 'You are my son whom I love, with you I am well pleased'.

If Jesus' ministry at this time was only just beginning, how could God be pleased at his baptism? Shouldn't he save it for when

---

[3] Jennifer Rees Larcombe, *Angel Called Mervyn*, Zondervan, 1999.

he had done all the wonderful things he would do in his life and death? God is actually more interested in who we are than in our performance.

When a new baby comes into the family, there is nothing the child can do for the parents apart from give them sleepless nights, make demands on them, and cause them worry, but the parents never stop talking about how wonderful the child is, how gorgeous the child is, what pleasure they have from having the child.

Martin Atkins once told a story during a sermon at Cliff College, when he was the principal, about a minister who visits an elderly couple. The old lady is very ill and is in bed. She has lost most of her hair, was frail, and her teeth were in a glass at the side of the bed. The minister knocked on the front door, and the old man let him in. He took him to the room where his wife was, and the old man turned to the minister and said, 'This is my wife, isn't she beautiful? Isn't she wonderful?'

What the old man saw was not what his wife couldn't be or couldn't do but who she was, his wife. He loved his wife, not what she could do for him.

I know my mum and dad were always supportive of the things we did, and they would make sure we had every opportunity they could possibly give us to experience new things. There was a time when I desperately wanted to learn to play the piano and the flute, but there was no way they could afford to buy me a flute or pay for piano lessons. Despite this and the fact that no-one in the family was musical, one day, hidden behind the settee was a box with a flute in it. My dad had bought it on HP and hid it to surprise me. He paid for that flute for years. He somehow managed to pay for piano lessons for me as well and for my other passion of swimming. He made sure my sister and I could be part of a good swimming club even though it cost him all his free time because his way of paying for the coaching fees was by coaching swimming himself as a volunteer.

I never made it as an Olympic swimmer or a famous musician, and when I stopped piano lessons and stopped swimming competitively, my dad never once told me it was a waste of money or that he regretted any of the sacrifice he'd made. He continued to support me throughout my life even when he didn't really understand what it was that I was doing or why.

There are no rules to unconditional love. Even though I always wanted to please him and loved making him happy and proud of me, my dad's love towards me wasn't dependent on whether I pleased or impressed him. He would have been just as delighted with me had I left school at 16 and got a job as he was when I got my degree.

God's nature is love, it never changes. We can't make him love us any more or any less by what we do. God accepts us and radically loves us (outrageous love). He embraces us and calls us his own.

My adopted friend had to learn to live with her new position as a child of her new mum and dad. Living with your God-given identity, even if you're different, you have been set free by the cross, free to be a child of God. Freedom as a Christian is not about being set free from the desire to love and please God. It is about being set free from the compulsion to earn God's love by doing things to please him.

Many of us in our prayer life are in danger of falling back into that slavery and praying as though we were slaves rather than children of God. We pray things like, 'Use me today', and we're desperate to earn the approval and favour of God. Begging daily to be used is not the language of a child of a loving parent.

In the film *Shrek*, you see this pitiful scene where Donkey is so desperate to be wanted and needed, he keeps shouting, 'Pick me! Pick me!' With God, we don't have to beg; he has already done that.

As children of our heavenly Father we can come to him confidently, gratefully, and expectantly, eager to get involved in his ongoing work rather than pleading for his attention. We can relax in his love and care and the knowledge that if we are walking with him, he will involve us in what he is doing.

My mum and dad always had confidence in me even though I let them down lots. When I went for my O-level results, I came back to a card that had been written before I even got the results, congratulating me on passing all ten. On the day that I did my driving test, when I got back my dad just handed over the keys to his car for me to go down to the shops and get my mum's paper. He never even asked me whether I had passed.

My dad knew there were times I didn't get it right, but he never allowed me to feel sorry for myself. It was always about, 'Well, there's nothing you can do about it, so you just have to get on with it'.

It is worth watching the film *Twelve Years a Slave,* which follows twelve years of a man who was forced into slavery in the US. At the end of the film the law changes and the slaves are given their freedom. But many could not handle the idea of freedom. Slavery is what they knew, and when asked what difference it had made to them being set free, in reality it made no difference because they still related the same way to their situations. They may have had a piece of paper that declared free, but in reality they weren't.

God does not send slaves to the Promised Land. It's reserved for the sons and daughters of the living God. We can experience Promised Land living only when we understand and get it straight that we are sons and daughters of a living God.

My friend's freedom came from knowing and believing that she had been set free to be the child of her new parents.

Points to Consider

1. Listen to 'Outrageous Love' (www.youtube.com/ watch?v=stGmBcwmDMQ). Within a group setting make a list of evidence of God's love for us. Then pray together and thank God for his outrageous love.

2. Many Christians reach physical and spiritual burnout because they spend their lives doing rather than being. In your local preacher's studies (in "Faith and Worship") you will look at "Being and Doing". There is a place for both. Look at the story of Martha and Mary in Luke 10:38–42, and then

compare their roles in the story of the raising of Lazarus (John 11). Which is the 'better thing'?

3. What are the things that stop you from being free to be a son or daughter or God?

CHAPTER 19

Thank You

THIS ADOPTIVE RELATIONSHIP between God and the believer brings the believer into the household of faith. For the Christian it is an amazing thing to know that they belong to the family of God for ever and ever. This is why God sent Jesus, his son, to die for the sins of his family, so we can be in relationship with him – so we can have the inheritance.

This Spirit not only cries out in making us a part of God's adopted family but gives believers blessings they never had before their adoption. Being the child of God is an experience like nothing else, and we often don't fully understand it even now because of how often the doctrine of adoption is overlooked. But when we see exactly what this adoption does for the believer and the blessings it provides, we can see that it is nothing but by the grace of God. From the moment the Spirit is poured into our hearts, this confidence of adoption is poured into us as well.

When we are adopted, 'The Spirit himself bears witness with our spirit that we are children of God' (Galatians 4:7). We can have a relationship with God because of this.

When we are adopted, not only do we have this relationship with God but also there is the blessing of the guidance of the Spirit that cries "Abba Father". This is how we know we are part of the family of God (Romans 8:15).

When we are adopted, it gives us another blessing. That this Spirit gives his presence to always assure the believer of their status as a child of God (Romans 8:16).

When we are adopted, the Christian heart is in perfect relationship with the Father, God (Romans 8:14).

When we are adopted, most of all, the privilege for the believer is that, at the point of adoption, they now become heirs of God, which is a joint heir with Christ (Romans 8:17).

When we are adopted, we have God's promise that one day we will bear the likeness of Christ (1 John 3:2).

Lastly, the blessing that the believer receives in adoption includes the inheritance of all things since the believer is adopted as a child of God (1 Corinthians 3:21–23).

This new relationship brings the believer into the household of faith. It's wonderful to know they will belong to this family forever. God will care for his family and take care of them for eternity. This is why God sent Jesus to die for the sins of his family – so we can have the best blessings, the inheritance, the spiritual richness of being part of the family of God.

When we help others in terms of discipleship classes and courses and preaching, it's important that we recognise that they are unique and individual and made special. They are fearfully and wonderfully, made and as Psalm 139:13–16 states,

> For you created my inmost being you knit me together in my mother womb. I praise you because I am fearfully and wonderfully made your works are wonderful, I know that full well. My frame was not hidden from you when I was made in the secret place. When I was woven together in the depths of the earth, your eyes saw my unformed body. All the days ordained for me were written in your book before one of them came to be.

God made them to be the people that he wanted them to be but then put them in a place where they could be nurtured and grow and learn how to become more like their heavenly Father as they mature.

While I have never adopted children myself, I know that adopting can be an expensive and costly process; there are solicitors, social workers, paperwork, red tape, and background checks; these things can cost money and are emotionally draining. While this is a hindrance, it won't scare away those potential parents who want it badly enough. If they really want that adoption to happen, they are willing to pay a heavy price.

Similarly, in order to make our adoption by God possible, there was a heavy price to pay. In the church that I attend I was recently reminded by an older member that when we take communion, we are reminded of the great price that was paid in order to make it possible for us to enter into a Father-child relationship with the God of the universe. The bread represents the broken body of Jesus, and the juice or wine symbolises his spilled blood. The price that had to be paid so that you and I could be adopted by God was the broken body and spilled blood of Jesus. This is why Jesus told his disciples (and by extension, us) to participate in the Lord's supper regularly: to remember what he did, the price that had to be paid.

There is no shortcut to listening to God – sons and daughters lean in, slow their pace, commune intentionally with their dad, and busy themselves doing exactly what the Father asks them to do.

God didn't mess up when he made us. God doesn't place his Spirit in mistakes. You're intentionally designed and wonderfully made.

We have an amazing God, a God we have the privilege of leading others to each week in our churches, a God who is the creator of the universe, but he is also a God who wants to have this adoptive personal relationship with his children.

My own adoption into my family is something I thank God for, something I believe was part of God's plan for me. I am forever thankful for his amazing love in allowing me to be born to someone who loved me enough to do the best she could for me, of giving me life and giving me to a family who could give me the love and security that I needed as I grew up. I'm thankful for the amazing love of a family who made me their own. But most of all I am grateful for the relationship that I have with a loving Father God who was willing to give everything to adopt me into his family.

When we are adopted, we gain the care of a family that includes us, encourages us, and emboldens us, trains us up in righteousness and gives us our identity and place of belonging.

My friend always calls her daughter 'Princess' and treats her like one. God sees us all in this way as princes and princesses, heirs to the kingdom, so we should start to live like we are princes and princesses. In a prayer meeting recently we were reminded if we keep our heads down, then the crowns that our Father has given us are likely to fall off. It's important that we walk in that knowledge that we are princess and princesses and are God's children, and that is something we can shout about!

Adoption Assures the Believer of God's Fatherly Electing Grace[4]

AT THE HEART of John Calvin's theology and undergirding his development of the *ordo salutis* is the doctrine of adoption. Many scholars note that Calvin does not treat adoption as a separate locus in his systematic theology and magnum opus, *The Institutes of the Christian Religion*. This is due in part to the fact that Calvin weaves the doctrine throughout the tapestry of God's marvellous work in the salvation of sinners. The doctrine of adoption is not peripheral, but rather central to Calvin's theology as noted by Sinclair Ferguson (*The Reformed Doctrine of Sonship, in Pulpit and People, Essays in Honour of William Still*) who writes, 'students of Calvin's theology have too rarely recognized how important the concept of Sonship was to his understanding of the Christian life'.

The fountainhead of adoption and its privileges in John Calvin's thought is found in God the Father. Specifically the privileges that the adopted child of God receives are the comfort of the Father's

---

[4] www.calvin500.com from *Calvin's Practical View of Adoption: Its Privileges and Duties.*

providence and the assurance received through the Father's electing grace.

One of those privileges is that *Adoption assures the believer of God's fatherly electing grace*. The electing grace of the Father almost becomes synonymous in Calvin's writings with the doctrine of adoption. He does not clearly delineate between these two concepts but rather merges them to show how adoption becomes a confirmation of election. Howard Griffith in his article clearly proves that election and adoption are closely tied in Calvin's thought when he states:

> It is quite clear that Calvin's intention was to use the biblical teaching on election as Scripture does: in the service of assurance for believers. Election was dangerous and only a snare when considered abstractly. But if for the sake of the analysis of Calvin's own thinking, we think of it first, it is fascinating to notice that Calvin repeatedly refers to election as God's *adoption* of the believer. This is not just the slip of a pen: Calvin repeats it often.

Adoption can be conceived of as the rear view mirror if you will, confirming the electing grace of the Father in the life of the believer. The close relationship of election and adoption serves to assure the believer that he is indeed a child of God.

In his *Sermons on Election and Reprobation*, Calvin closely links election and adoption when he says, 'So, when our Lord engraved his fear in our hearts by his holy Spirit, and such an obedience towards him, as his Children ought to perform unto him, this is as if he should set upon us the seal of his election, and as if he should truly testify that he hath adopted us and that he is a Father unto us'. Throughout the *Institutes* he makes several references to the close relation between election and adoption where free election by the grace of God becomes the ground of the believer's adoption. He states, 'We were adopted in Christ into the eternal inheritance because in ourselves we were not capable of such great excellence'.

Furthermore, man cannot renovate himself to receive the adoption of sons, nor is adoption because of any foreseen merit on God's part, because 'God's special election towers and rules over all, alone ratifying his adoption'.

This assurance of election is further buttressed in his *Sermons on Ephesians* where he says, 'When he [Paul] says that God has predestined us by adoption, it is to show that if we be God's children it is not through nature but through his pure grace ... for we have no such status by birth or inheritance, neither does it come of flesh and blood'. The assurance this affords the believer is that it is by the grace of God in Jesus Christ that they are adopted into the family of God and thus 'they whom he calls to salvation ought not to seek the cause of it anywhere else than in this gratuitous adoption'. Calvin continues speaking of the assurance that election and adoption affords the believer:

Whosoever then believes is thereby assured that God has worked in him, and faith, as it were, the duplicate copy that God gives us of the original of our adoption.... It follows then that if we have faith, we are also adopted. For why does God gives us faith? Even because he elected us before the creation of the world. This therefore is an infallible order that insofar as the faithful receive God's grace and embrace his mercy, holding Jesus Christ as their Head, to obtain salvation in this way, they know assuredly that God has adopted them.

Far from declaring God's election to be cold, calculating and deterministic, Calvin ties election and adoption closely together showing the comfort and warmth that can be derived from doing so. Election becomes the ground of adoption, and thus offers assurance to the child of God that he really is one of God's children. The root of adoption is not found in the believer, but in God the Father, through Jesus Christ.

APPENDIX 2

Ames's Differences between Human and Divine Adoption⁵

WILLIAM AMES SAYS there are four differences between human and divine adoption:

1. Human adoption relates to a person, who, as a stranger, has no right to the inheritance except through adoption. But believers, though by natural birth they have no right to the inheritance of life, are given it because of rebirth, faith, and justification.

2. Human adoption is only an outward designation and bestowal of external things. But divine adoption is so real a relationship that it is based on an inward action and the communications of a new inner life.

3. Human adoption was introduced when there were no, or too few, natural sons. But divine adoption is not from any want

⁵ http://gospelcenteredmusings.com/2013/09/10/
amess-differences-between-human-divine-adoption/.

but from abundant goodness, whereby a likeness of a natural son and mystical union is given to the adopted sons.

4. The human adoption is ordained so that the son may succeed the father in the inheritance. But divine adoption is not ordained for succession, but for participation in the inheritance assigned. Both the Father and his first-begotten Son live forever and this admits no succession

APPENDIX 3

People Who Were Adopted in the Bible

Moses

In Exodus 2:10, we read: 'Pharaoh had ordered the midwives to kill all of the Hebrew baby boys when they were born, so Moses' mother hid her baby for three months. The mother placed baby Moses in a basket where Pharaoh's daughter bathed in the Nile. Pharaoh's daughter found the baby, adopted him, and raised Moses as her son'.

Exodus 2 says, 'Later, when the boy was older, his mother brought him back to Pharaoh's daughter, who adopted him as her own son. The princess named him Moses, for she explained, "I lifted him out of the water"'.

Esther

In Esther 2:7, we read: 'This man had a very beautiful and lovely young cousin, Hadassah, who was also called Esther. When her father and mother died, Mordecai adopted her into his family and raised her as his own daughter'.

Here is the quote from Esther 2:7: 'He had brought up Hadassah that is Esther, the daughter of his uncle, for she had neither father nor mother; the maiden was beautiful and lovely'.

Ruth

Ruth was esteemed by her mother-in-law, Naomi, but was really viewed more like a daughter. Naomi would refer to Ruth as 'my daughter' (see Ruth 3:16–18.) When Ruth had a baby, she laid the baby on Naomi's lap as a symbol of Naomi adopting the baby:

So Boaz took Ruth and she became his wife. Then he went to her, and the Lord enabled her to conceive, and she gave birth to a son … Then Naomi took the child, laid him in her lap and cared for him. The women living there said, "Naomi has a son' (Ruth 4:13, 16–17).

Jacob's children

Adopting babies appears much earlier in the Bible than even these stories. When Jacob married two sisters, sibling rivalry ran amuck. Jacob loved Rachel more, but Leah bore him children while Rachel was barren. So Rachel told Jacob to 'lie with' her handmaiden, and Rachel adopted her children: So [Rachel] gave [Jacob] her servant Bilhah as a wife. Jacob slept with her, and she became pregnant and bore him a son. Then Rachel said, 'God has vindicated me; he has listened to my plea and given me a son'. Because of this she named him Dan (Genesis 30:4–6).

Jesus' lineage

What really drives home adoption in the Bible is the story of Jesus' lineage. Even though God had very strict standards for the Jews, he 'adopted' different Gentiles into the lineage of King David and, in turn, Jesus himself. Rahab the harlot was 'adopted' into the Jewish tribe, giving birth to Boaz, who married another 'adopted' Gentile, Ruth. While neither of these women was Jewish, they were esteemed for their faith and considered worthy enough to be part of Jesus' lineage.

Jesus' lineage captures what adoption is all about. It did not matter where these women were born. What matters is that they became part of the family. Not only were they part of the family, they were important enough to be two of the very few women mentioned in Jesus' lineage, which is saying something in a culture that did not value women.

Jesus

Jesus was also technically involved in step-parent adoption because God himself was the father. Mary was already pregnant with Jesus when she married Joseph. Joseph, who was a carpenter, raised Jesus as his son, and Jesus was known as 'the carpenter's son' (see Matthew 13:53–57).

Even Jesus saw others as his 'mother and brothers' who were not blood relatives. He defined this relationship in a different way:

> Then Jesus' mother and brothers arrived. Standing outside, they sent someone in to call him. A crowd was sitting around him, and they told him, 'Your mother and brothers are outside looking for you'. 'Who are my mother and my brothers?' he asked. Then he looked at those seated in a circle around him and said, 'Here are my mother and my brothers! Whoever does God's will is my brother and sister and mother?' (Mark 3:31–34)

Wesley's Sermon No 9

'The Spirit of Bondage and of Adoption'

Ye have not received the spirit of bondage again unto fear; but ye have received the Spirit of adoption, whereby we cry Abba, Father.—Romans 8:15

1. St Paul here speaks to those who are the children of God by faith. 'Ye', saith he, who are indeed his children, have drank into his Spirit; 'ye have not received the spirit of bondage again unto fear'; 'but, because ye are sons, God hath sent forth the Spirit of his Son into your hearts'. 'Ye have received the Spirit of adoption, whereby we cry, Abba, Father'.

2. The spirit of bondage and fear is widely distant from this loving Spirit of adoption: Those who are influenced only by slavish fear, cannot be termed 'the sons of God'; yet some of them may be styled his servants, and are 'not far from the kingdom of heaven'.

3. But it is to be feared, the bulk of mankind, yea, of what is called the Christian world, have not attained even this; but are still afar off, 'neither is God in all their thoughts'. A few names may be found of those who love God; a few more there

are that fear him; but the greater part have neither the fear of God before their eyes, nor the love of God in their hearts.

4. Perhaps most of you, who, by the mercy of God, now partake of a better spirit, may remember the time when ye were as they, when ye were under the same condemnation. But at first ye knew it not, though ye were wallowing daily in your sins and in your blood; till, in due time, ye 'received the spirit of fear'; (ye received, for this also is the gift of God;) and afterwards, fear vanished away, and the Spirit of love filled your hearts.

5. One who is in the first state of mind, without fear of love, is in Scripture termed a 'natural man': One who is under the spirit of bondage and fear, is sometimes said to be 'under the law': (Although that expression more frequently signifies one who is under the Jewish dispensation, or who thinks himself obliged to observe all the rites and ceremonies of the Jewish law:) But one who has exchanged the spirit of fear for the Spirit of love, is properly said to be 'under grace'.

Now, because it highly imports us to know what spirit we are of, I shall endeavour to point out distinctly, First, the state of a 'natural man': Secondly, that of one who is 'under the law': And Thirdly, of one who is 'under grace'.

I.

1. And, First, the state of a natural man. This the Scripture represents as a state of sleep: The voice of God to him is, 'Awake thou that sleepest'. For his soul is in a deep sleep: His spiritual senses are not awake; They discern neither spiritual good nor evil. The eyes of his understanding are closed; They are sealed together, and see not. Clouds and darkness continually rest upon them; for he lies in the valley of the shadow of death. Hence having no inlets for the knowledge of spiritual things, all the avenues of his soul being shut up, he

is in gross, stupid ignorance of whatever he is most concerned to know. He is utterly ignorant of God, knowing nothing concerning him as he ought to know. He is totally a stranger to the law of God, as to its true, inward, spiritual meaning. He has no conception of that evangelical holiness, without which no man shall see the Lord; nor of the happiness which they only find whose 'life is hid with Christ in God'.

2. And for this very reason, because he is fast asleep, he is, in some sense, at rest. Because he is blind, he is also secure; He saith, 'Tush, there shall no harm happen unto me'. The darkness which covers him on every side, keeps him in a kind of peace; so far as peace can consist with the works of the devil, and with an earthly, devilish mind. He sees not that he stands on the edge of the pit, therefore he fears it not. He cannot tremble at the danger he does not know. He has not understanding enough to fear. Why is it that he is in no dread of God Because he is totally ignorant of him: If not saying in his heart, 'There is no God'; or, that 'he sitteth on the circle of the heavens, and humbleth' not 'himself to behold the things which are done on earth': yet satisfying himself as well to all Epicurean intents and purposes, by saying, 'God is merciful'; confounding and swallowing up all at once in that unwieldy idea of mercy, all his holiness and essential hatred of sin; all his justice, wisdom, and truth. He is in no dread of the vengeance denounced against those who obey not the blessed law of God, because he understands it not. He imagines the main point is to do thus, to be outwardly blameless; and sees not that it extends to every temper, desire, thought, motion of the heart. Or he fancies that the obligation hereto is ceased; that Christ came to 'destroy the Law and the Prophets'; to save his people in, not from their sins; to bring them to heaven without holiness: – Notwithstanding his own words, 'Not one jot or tittle of the law shall pass away, till all things are fulfilled'; and 'Not every one that saith unto me, Lord,

Lord! shall enter into the kingdom of heaven; but he that doeth the will of my Father which is in heaven'.

3. He is secure, because he is utterly ignorant of himself. Hence he talks of 'repenting by and by'; he does not indeed exactly know when, but some time or other before he dies; taking it for granted, that this is quite in his own power. For what should hinder his doing it, if he will if he does but once set a resolution, no fear but he will make it good!

4. But this ignorance never so strongly glares, as in those who are termed, men of learning. If a natural man be one of these, he can talk at large of his rational faculties, of the freedom of his will, and the absolute necessity of such freedom, in order to constitute man a moral agent. He reads, and argues, and proves to a demonstration, that every man may do as he will; may dispose his own heart to evil or good, as it seems best in his own eyes. Thus the god of this world spreads a double veil of blindness over his heart, lest, by any means, 'the light of the glorious gospel of Christ should shine' upon it.

5. From the same ignorance of himself and God, there may sometimes arise, in the natural man, a kind of joy, in congratulating himself upon his own wisdom and goodness: And what the world calls joy, he may often possess. He may have pleasure in various kinds; either in gratifying the desires of the flesh, or the desire of the eye, or the pride of life; particularly if he has large possessions; if he enjoy an affluent fortune; then he may 'clothe' himself 'in purple and fine linen, and fare sumptuously every day'. And so long as he thus doeth well unto himself, men will doubtless speak good of him. They will say, 'He is a happy man'. For, indeed, this is the sum of worldly happiness; to dress, and visit, and talk, and eat, and drink, and rise up to play.

6. It in not surprising, if one in such circumstances as these, dosed with the opiates of flattery and sin, should imagine, among his other waking dreams, that he walks in great liberty. How easily may he persuade himself, that he is at liberty from

all vulgar errors, and from the prejudice of education; judging exactly right, and keeping clear of all extremes. 'I am free', may he say, 'from all the enthusiasm of weak and narrow souls; from superstition, the disease of fools and cowards, always righteous over much; and from bigotry, continually incident to those who have not a free and generous way of thinking'. And too sure it is, that he is altogether free from the 'wisdom which cometh from above', from holiness, from the religion of the heart, from the whole mind which was in Christ.

7. For all this time he is the servant of sin. He commits sin, more or less, day by day. Yet he is not troubled: He 'is in no bondage', as some speak; he feels no condemnation. He contents himself (even though he should profess to believe that the Christian Revelation is of God) with, 'Man is frail. We are all weak. Every man has his infirmity'. Perhaps he quotes Scripture: 'Why, does not Solomon say, – The righteous man falls into sin seven times a day! – And, doubtless, they are all hypocrites or enthusiasts who pretend to be better than their neighbours'. If, at any time, a serious thought fix upon him, he stifles it as soon as possible, with, 'Why should I fear, since God is merciful, and Christ died for sinners' Thus, he remains a willing servant of sin, content with the bondage of corruption; inwardly and outwardly unholy, and satisfied therewith; not only not conquering sin, but not striving to conquer, particularly that sin which doth so easily beset him.

8. Such is the state of every natural man; whether he be a gross, scandalous transgressor, or a more reputable and decent sinner, having the form, though not the power of godliness. But how can such an one be convinced of sin? How is he brought to repent to be under the law to receive the spirit of bondage unto fear? This is the point which is next to be considered.

II.

1. By some awful providence, or by his word applied with the demonstration of his Spirit, God touches the heart of him that lay asleep in darkness and in the shadow of death. He is terribly shaken out of his sleep, and awakes into a consciousness of his danger. Perhaps in a moment, perhaps by degrees, the eyes of his understanding are opened, and now first (the veil being in part removed) discern the real state he is in. Horrid light breaks in upon his soul; such light, as may be conceived to gleam from the bottomless pit, from the lowest deep, from a lake of fire burning with brimstone. He at last sees the loving, the merciful God is also 'a consuming fire'; that he is a just God and a terrible, rendering to every man according to his words, entering into judgment with the ungodly for every idle word, yea, and for the imaginations of the heart. He now clearly perceives, that the great and holy God is 'of purer eyes than to behold iniquity'; that he is an avenger of every one who rebelleth against him, and repayeth the wicked to his face; and that 'it is a fearful thing to fall into the hands of the living God'.

2. The inward, spiritual meaning of the law of God now begins to glare upon him. He perceives 'the commandment is exceeding broad', and there is 'nothing hid from the light thereof'. He is convinced, that every part of it relates, not barely to outward sin or obedience, but to what passes in the secret recesses of the soul, which no eye but God's can penetrate. If he now hears, 'Thou shalt not kill', God speaks in thunder, 'He that hateth his brother is a murderer'; 'he that saith unto his brother, Thou fool, is obnoxious to hell-fire'. If the law say, 'Thou shalt not commit adultery', the voice of the Lord sounds in his ears, 'He that looketh on a woman to lust after her hath committed adultery with her already in his heart'. And thus, in every point, he feels the word of God 'quick and powerful, sharper than a two-edged sword'.

It 'pierces even to the dividing asunder of his soul and spirit, his joints and marrow'. And so much the more, because he is conscious to himself of having neglected so great salvation; of having 'trodden under foot the son of God', who would have saved him from his sins, and 'counted the blood of the covenant an unholy', a common, unsanctifying thing.

3. And as he knows, 'all things are naked and open unto the eyes of him with whom we have to do', so he sees himself naked, stripped of all the fig-leaves which he had sewed together, of all his poor pretences to religion or virtue, and his wretched excuses for sinning against God. He now sets himself like the ancient sacrifices, cleft in sunder, as it were, from the neck downward, so that all within him stands confessed. His heart is bare, and he sees it is all sin, 'deceitful above all things, desperately wicked'; that it is altogether corrupt and abominable, more than it is possible for tongue to express; that there dwelleth therein no good thing, but unrighteousness and ungodliness only; every motion thereof, every temper and thought, being only evil continually.

4. And he not only sees, but feels in himself, by an emotion of soul which he cannot describe, that for the sins of his heart were his life without blame, (which yet it is not, and cannot be; seeing 'an evil tree cannot bring forth good fruit',) he deserves to be cast into the fire that never shall be quenched. He feels that 'the wages', the just reward 'of sin', of his sin above all, 'is death'; even the second death; the death which dieth not; the destruction of body and soul in hell.

5. Here ends his pleasing dream, his delusive rest, his false peace, his vain security. His joy now vanishes as a cloud; pleasures, once loved, delight no more. They pall upon the taste: He loathes the nauseous sweet; he is weary to bear them. The shadows of happiness flee away, and sink into oblivion: So that he is stripped of all, and wanders to and fro, seeking rest, but finding none.

6. The fumes of those opiates being now dispelled, he feels the anguish of a wounded spirit. He finds that sin let loose upon the soul (whether it be pride, anger, or evil desire, whether self-will, malice, envy, revenge, or any other) is perfect misery: He feels sorrow of heart for the blessings he has lost, and the curse which is come upon him: remorse for having thus destroyed himself, and despised his own mercies; fear, from a lively sense of the wrath of God, and of the consequences of his wrath, of the punishment which he has justly deserved, and which he sees hanging over is head; – fear of death, as being to him the gate of hell, the entrance of death eternal; – fear of the devil, the executioner of the wrath and righteous vengeance of God; – fear of men, who, if they were able to kill his body, would thereby plunge both body and soul into hell; fear, sometimes arising to such a height, that the poor, sinful, guilty soul, is terrified with everything, with nothing, with shades, with a leaf shaken of the wind. Yea, sometimes it may even border upon distraction, making a man 'drunken though not with wine', suspending the exercise of the memory, of the understanding, of all the natural faculties. Sometimes it may approach to the very brink of despair; so that he who trembles at the name of death, may yet be ready to plunge into it every moment, to 'choose strangling rather than life'. Well may such a man roar, like him of old, for the very disquietness of his heart. Well may he cry out, 'The spirit of a man may sustain his infirmities; but a wounded spirit who can bear'

7. Now he truly desires to break loose from sin, and begins to struggle with it. But though he strive with all his might, he cannot conquer: Sin is mightier than he. He would fain escape; but he is so fast in prison, that he cannot get forth. He resolved against sin, but yet sins on: He sees the snare, and abhors, and runs into it. So much does his boasted reason avail, – only to enhance his guilt, and increase his misery! Such is the freedom of his will; free only to evil; free to 'drink

in iniquity like water'; to wander farther and farther from the living God, and do more 'despite to the Spirit of grace!'

8.   The more he strive, wishes, labours to be free, the more does he feel his chains, the grievous chains of sin, wherewith Satan binds and 'leads him captive at his will'; his servant he is, though he repine ever so much; though he rebel, he cannot prevail. He is still in bondage and fear, by reason of sin: Generally, of some outward sin, to which he is peculiarly disposed, either, by nature, custom, or outward circumstance; but always, of some inward sin, some evil temper or unholy affection. And the more he frets against it, the more it prevails; he may bite but cannot break his chain. Thus he toils without end, repenting and sinning, and repenting and sinning again, till at length the poor, sinful, helpless wretch is even at his wit's end and can barely groan, 'O wretched man that I am! who shall deliver me from the body of this death'

9.   This whole struggle of one who is 'under the law', under the 'spirit of fear and bondage', is beautifully described by the Apostle in the foregoing chapter, speaking in the person of an awakened man. 'I', saith he, 'was alive without the law once': (Verse 9:) I had much life, wisdom, strength, and virtue; so I thought: 'But, when the commandment came, sin revived, and I died': When the commandment, in its spiritual meaning, came to my heart, with the power of God, my inbred sin was stirred up, fretted, inflamed, and all my virtue died away. 'And the commandment, which was ordained to life, I found to be unto death. For sin taking occasion by the commandment, deceived me, and by it slew me': (Verses 10,11:) It came upon me unaware; slew all my hopes; and plainly showed, in the midst of life I was in death. 'Wherefore the law is holy, and the commandment holy, and just, and good': (Verse 12:) I no longer lay the blame on this, but on the corruption of my own heart. I acknowledge that 'the law is spiritual; but I am carnal, sold under sin': (Verse 14:) I now see both the spiritual nature of the law; and my own carnal,

devilish heart 'sold under sin', totally enslaved: (Like slaves bought with money, who were absolutely at their master's disposal:) 'For that which I do, I allow not; for what I would, I do not, but what I hate, that I do': (Verse 15:) Such is the bondage under which I groan; such the tyranny of my hard master. 'To will is present with me, but how to perform that which is good I find not. For the good that I would, I do not; but the evil which I would not, that I do': (Verses 18, 19:) 'I find a law', an inward constraining power, 'that when I would do good, evil is present with me. For I delight in 'or consent to 'the law of God, after the inward man': (Verses 21, 22:) In my 'mind': (So the apostle explains himself in the words that immediately follow; and so, o esv anqrvpos, the inward man, is understood in all other Greek writers:) 'But I see another law in my members', another constraining power, 'warring against the law of my mind', or inward man, 'and bringing me into captivity to the law' or power 'of sin': (Verse 23:) Dragging me, as it were, at my conqueror's chariot-wheels, into the very thing which my soul abhors. 'O wretched man that I am! who shall deliver me from the body of this death' (Verse 24.) Who shall deliver me from this helpless, dying life, from this bondage of sin and misery Till this is done, 'I myself' (or rather, that I, autos egv, that man I am now personating) 'with the mind', or inward man, 'serve the law of God'; my mind, my conscience is on God's side; 'but with my flesh', with my body, 'the law of sin' (verse 25,) being hurried away by a force I cannot resist.

10. How lively a portraiture is this of one 'under the law'; one who feels the burden he cannot shake off; who pants after liberty, power, and love, but is in fear and bondage still! until the time that God answers the wretched man, crying out, 'Who shall deliver me' from this bondage of sin, from this body of death – 'The grace of God, through Jesus Christ thy Lord'.

III.

1. Them it is that this miserable bondage ends, and he is no more 'under the law, but under grace'. This state we are, Thirdly, to consider; the state of one who has found grace or favour in the sight of God, even the Father, and who has the grace or power of the Holy Ghost, reigning in his heart; who has received, in the language of the Apostle, the 'Spirit of adoption, whereby' he now cries, 'Abba, Father!'

2. 'He cried unto the Lord in his trouble, and God delivers him out of his distress'. His eyes are opened in quite another manner than before, even to see a loving, gracious God. While he is calling, 'I beseech thee, show me thy glory!' – he hears a voice in the inmost soul, 'I will make all my goodness pass before thee, and I will proclaim the name of the Lord: I will be gracious to whom I will be gracious, and I will show mercy to whom I will show mercy'. And, it is not long before 'the Lord' descends in the cloud, and proclaims the name of the Lord'. Then he sees, but not with eyes of flesh and blood, 'The Lord, the Lord God, merciful and gracious, long-suffering, and abundant in goodness and truth; keeping mercy for thousands, and forgiving iniquities, and transgressions and sin'.

3. Heavenly, healing light now breaks in upon his soul. He 'looks on him whom he had pierced'; and 'God, who out of darkness commanded light to shine, shineth in his heart'. He sees the light of the glorious love of God, in the face of Jesus Christ. He hath a divine 'evidence of things not seen' by sense, even of the 'deep things of God'; more particularly of the love of God, of his pardoning love to him that believes in Jesus. Overpowered with the sight, his whole soul cried out, 'My Lord and my God'; For he sees all his iniquities laid on Him, who 'bare them in his own body on the tree'; he beholds the Lamb of God taking away his sins. How clearly now does he discern, that 'God was in Christ, reconciling the world

unto himself; making him sin for us, who knew no sin, that we might be made the righteousness of God through him'; – and that he himself is reconciled to God, by that blood of the covenant!

5. Here end both the guilt and power of sin. He can now say, 'I am crucified with Christ: Nevertheless I live; yet not I but Christ liveth in me: And the life which I now live in the flesh', (even in this mortal body,) 'I live by faith in the Son of God, who loved me, and gave himself for me'. Here end remorse, and sorrow of heart, and the anguish of a wounded spirit. 'God turneth his heaviness into joy'. He made sore, and now his hands bind up. Here ends also that bondage unto fear; for 'his heart standeth fast, believing in the Lord'. He cannot fear any longer the wrath of God; for he knows it is now turned away from him, and looks upon Him no more as an angry Judge, but as a loving Father. He cannot fear the devil, knowing he has 'no power, except it be given him from above'. He fears not hell; being an heir of the kingdom of heaven: Consequently, he has no fear of death; by reason whereof he was in time past, for so many years, 'subject to bondage'. Rather, knowing that 'if the earthly house of this tabernacle be dissolved, he hath a building of God, a house not made with hands, eternal in the heavens; he groaneth earnestly, desiring to be clothed upon with that house which is from heaven'. He groans to shake off this house of earth, that 'mortality' may be 'swallowed up of life'; knowing that God 'hath wrought him for the self-same thing; who hath also given him the earnest of his Spirit'.

6. And 'where the Spirit of the Lord is, there is liberty'; liberty, not only from guilt and fear, but from sin, from that heaviest of all yokes, that basest of all bondage. His labour is not now in vain. The snare is broken, and he is delivered. He not only strives, but likewise prevails; he not only fights, but conquers also. 'Henceforth he does not serve sin'. (Chap. 6:6 &c.) He is 'dead unto sin, and alive unto God'; 'sin doth not now reign',

even 'in his mortal body', nor doth he 'obey it in the desires thereof'. He does not 'yield his members as instruments of unrighteousness unto sin, but as instruments of righteousness unto God'. For 'being now made free from sin, he is become the servant of righteousness'.

7. Thus, 'having peace with God, through our Lord Jesus Christ', 'rejoicing in hope of the glory of God', and having power over all sin, over every evil desire, and temper, and word, and work, he is a living witness of the 'glorious liberty of the sons of God'; all of whom, being partakers of like precious faith, bear record with one voice, 'We have received the Spirit of adoption, whereby we cry, Abba, Father!'

8. It is this spirit which continually, 'worketh in them, both to will and to do of his good pleasure'. It is he that sheds the love of God abroad in their heart, and the love of all mankind; thereby purifying their hearts from the love of world, from the lust of the flesh, the lust of the eye, and the pride of life. It is by him they are delivered from anger and pride, from all vile and inordinate affections. In consequence, they are delivered from evil words and works, from all unholiness of conversation; doing no evil to any child of man, and being zealous of all good works.

9. To sum up all: the natural man neither fears nor loves God; one under the law, fears, – one under grace, loves him. The first has no light in the things of God, but walks in utter darkness; the second sees the painful light of hell; the third, the joyous light of heaven. He that sleeps in death, has a false peace; he that is awakened, has no peace at all; he that believes, has true peace, – the peace of God filling and ruling his heart. The Heathen, baptized or unbaptized, hath a fancied liberty, which is indeed licentiousness; the Jew, or one under the Jewish dispensation, is in heavy, grievous bondage; the Christian enjoys the true glorious liberty of the sons of God. An unawakened child of the devil sins willingly, one that is awakened sins unwillingly; a child of God 'sinneth not',

but 'keepeth himself, and the wicked one toucheth him not'. To conclude: the natural man neither conquers nor fights; the man under the law fights with sin, but cannot conquer; the man under grace fights and conquers, yea, is 'more than conqueror, through him that loveth him'.

IV.

1. From this plain account of the three-fold state of man, the natural, the legal, and the evangelical, it appears that it is not sufficient to divide mankind into sincere and insincere. A man may be sincere in any of these states; not only when he has the 'Spirit of adoption', but while he has the 'spirit of bondage unto fear'; yea, while he has neither this fear, nor love. For undoubtedly there may be sincere Heathens, as well as sincere Jews, or Christians. This circumstance, them does by no means prove that a man is in a state of acceptance with God.

'Examine yourselves, therefore', not only whether ye are sincere, but 'whether ye be in the faith'. Examine narrowly, (for it imports you much,) what is the ruling principle in your soul! Is it the love of God? Is it the fear of God? Or is it neither one nor the other? Is it not rather the love of the world the love of pleasure, or gain of ease, or reputation? If so, you are not come so far as a Jew. You are but a Heathen still. Have you heaven in your heart Have you the Spirit of adoption, ever crying, Abba, Father Or do you cry unto God, as 'out of the belly of hell', overwhelmed with sorrow and fear Or are you a stranger to this whole affair, and cannot imagine what I mean Heathen, pull off the mask! Thou hast never put on Christ! Stand barefaced! Look up to heaven; and own before Him that liveth for ever and ever, thou hast no part, either among the sons of servants of God!

Whosoever thou art: Dost thou commit sin, or dost thou not If thou dost, is it willingly, or unwillingly In either case, God hath told thee whose thou art: 'He that committeth sin is of the devil'. If thou committest it willingly, thou art his faithful servant: He will not fail to reward thy labour. If unwillingly, still thou art his servant. God deliver thee out of his hands!

Art thou daily fighting against all sin And daily more than conqueror I acknowledge thee for a child of God. O stand fast in thy glorious liberty! Art thou fighting, but not conquering striving for the mastery, but not able to attain Then thou art not yet a believer in Christ; but follow on, and thou shalt know the Lord. Art thou not fighting at all, but leading an easy, indolent, fashionable life! O how hast thou dared to name the name of Christ, only to make it a reproach among the Heathen Awake, thou sleeper! Call upon thy God before the deep swallow thee up!

2. Perhaps one reason why so many think of themselves more highly than they ought to think, why they do not discern what state they are in, is because these several states of soul are often mingled together, and in some measure meet in one and the same person. Thus experience shows, that the legal state, or state of fear, is frequently mixed with the natural; for few men are so fast asleep in sin, but they are sometimes more or less awakened. As the Spirit of God does not 'wait for the call of man', so, at some times he will be heard. He puts them in fear, so that, for a season at least, the Heathen 'know themselves to be but men'. They feel the burden of sin, and earnestly desire to flee from the wrath to come. But not long: They seldom suffer the arrows of conviction to go deep into their souls; but quickly stifle the grace of God, and return to their wallowing in the mire.

In like manner, the evangelical state, or state of love, is frequently mixed with the legal. For few of those who have the spirit of bondage and fear, remain always without hope. The wise and gracious God rarely suffers this; 'for he remembereth that we are but dust'; and he willeth not that 'the flesh should fail before him, or the spirit which he hath made'. Therefore, at such times as he seeth good, he gives a dawning of light unto them that sit in darkness. He causes a part of his goodness to pass before them, and shows he is a 'God that heareth the prayer'. They see the promise, which is by faith in Christ Jesus, though it be yet afar off; and hereby they are encouraged to 'run with patience the race which is set before them'.

3. Another reason why many deceive themselves is because they do not consider how far a man may go, and yet be in a natural, or, at best, a legal state. A man may be of a compassionate and a benevolent temper; he may be affable, courteous, generous, friendly; he may have some degree of meekness, patience, temperance, and of many other moral virtues. He may feel many desires of shaking off all vice, and of attaining higher degrees of virtue. He may abstain from much evil; perhaps from all that is grossly contrary to justice, mercy, or truth. He may do much good, may feed the hungry, clothe the naked, relieve the widow and fatherless. He may attend public worship, use prayer in private, read many books of devotion; and yet, for all this, he may be a mere natural man, knowing neither himself nor God; equally a stranger to the spirit of fear and to that of love; having neither repented, nor believed the gospel.

But suppose there were added to all this a deep conviction of sin, with much fear of the wrath of God; vehement desires to cast off every sin, and to fulfill all righteousness; frequent rejoicing in hope, and touches of love often glancing upon the soul; yet neither do these prove a man to be under grace;

to have true, living, Christian faith, unless the Spirit of adoption abide in his heart, unless he can continually cry, 'Abba, Father!'

4. Beware, then, thou who art called by the name of Christ, that thou come not short of the mark of thy high calling. Beware thou rest, not, either in a natural state with too many that are accounted good Christians; or in a legal state, wherein those who are highly esteemed of men are generally content to live and die. Nay, but God hath prepared better things for thee, if thou follow on till thou attain. Thou art not called to fear and tremble like devils; but to rejoice and love, like the angels of God. 'Thou shalt love the lord thy God will all thy heart, and with all thy soul, and with all thy mind, and with all thy strength'. Thou shalt 'rejoice evermore'; thou shalt 'pray without ceasing': thou shalt 'in everything give thanks'. Thou shalt do the will of God on earth as it is done in heaven. O prove thou 'what is that good, and acceptable, and perfect will of God!' Now present thyself 'a living sacrifice, holy, acceptable to God'. 'Whereunto thou hast already attained, hold fast', by 'reaching forth unto those things which are before': until 'the God of peace make thee perfect in every good work, working in thee that which is well-pleasing in his sight through Jesus Christ: To whom be glory for ever and ever! Amen!'

NOTES: SOME FINAL THOUGHTS FOR THOSE WHO WERE ADOPTED

THERE ARE SOME very well documented psychological effects of being adopted. For some, help may be needed in working through these issues.

These issues can stay with some people all the way through their lives. However, some of these issues are similar for people who are not adopted.

If you are an adopted child, it's important to remember that the circumstances of your adoption do not define you for the rest of your life. You are given a new life.

So many people have said to me that even though I wouldn't realize it at the time, the separation from my birth mother would have been traumatic for me as a baby and subconsciously, I would still have that insecurity.

Earlier this year, when I was thinking about this, I asked God to deal with this if this was an issue and to make it clear to me that he was dealing with it. Shortly after this, I was praying, and I could see myself as a baby with my birth mother. She was heartbroken and crying, but there was a wonderful sense that God had his arms wrapped round her. There was that same picture of me being loved and surrounded by love and being held as I was passed over to people I didn't know. But the hands that held me never let go. There wasn't a sense of insecurity in terms of where I came from or where I was going to, just that sense of being held and loved by God, who never let go of me.

Many people try to tell me that I have problems because of my lack of trust and not being able to find security in other people or things. I don't think it's totally to do with my adoption because there are people who have let me down throughout my life, and there have been disappointments on the way. Other people have had far more problems than I have even though they are not adopted. But what it points to is that even at that young age, God was teaching me that there is no security to be found in anything or in anybody apart from him. The only thing that matters is that we know we are secure in the Father's love and that he can be trusted 100 per cent. I know this to be true. Things don't always happen how I want them to happen, but God has never let me down, has never let go of me. He's promised in the Bible that he never will (e.g. Isaiah 31:10 and Hebrews 13:5). He gives those promises to all his children.

As an adopted child, it is important not to allow people to lead you to believe that everything you do is defined by what happened to you as a baby or a child. God has given you these experiences and can use them for his glory. Look at them through God's eyes. God transforms our experiences and does amazing things with them.

Being adopted is something to be celebrated; I'm blessed because I can celebrate my physical adoption as a child and my spiritual adoption as a child of God, as a Christian. On both occasions I was adopted by an awesome father!

BIBLIOGRAPHY

Beeke, JR, *Heirs with Christ: The puritans on Adoption*, Grand Rapids, MI: Heritage Books, 2008.

Boyde, B., *Sons and Daughters*, Zondervan, USA, 2012.

Christensen, DA, *The Spiritual Life of a Normal Christian Transformed by Adoption*, Maine, 2014.

Frost, J., *Spiritual Slavery to Spiritual Sonship*, Destiny Publishing, USA, 2006.

Holley, J and M, *Adopted by God*, Dorrance Publishing USA, 2008.

Jordan, J., *Sonship Tree of Life* New Zealand: Media, 2012.

Larcombe, JR, *Angel Called Mervyn*, Zondervan, UK, 1999.

Manning, B., *Abba's Child*, Colorado: NavPress, 2002.

Thomas, W., *Walking with God as Father*, Weybridge: New Wine Press, 2013.

Thompson, RB, *Groaning for Adoption*, Trumpet Ministries, USA, 2011.

Wesley, J., *John Wesley's Forty-Four Sermons*, Hargreaves Publishing, 1787.

Wesley, J. and C., *A collection of Hymns for the Use of the people called Methodists*

Wong, BCS, *The Call to Sonship*, Xulonpress, USA, 2011.

Useful Website
www.fatherhousetrust.com.

Printed in the United States
By Bookmasters